Thirty Questions Regarding the History of Pre-Stockport, Ohio

Thirty Questions Regarding the History of Pre-Stockport, Ohio

by

Gale Richard Walker, Ph.D.

2024

No part of this publication may be reproduced or transmitted in any form or by any means, electronic or technical, including photocopying, recording, or by any information storage or retrieval system, without permission in writing from the author or his heirs. However, copying, reproducing, and transmitting up to 50 pages of this publication for personal, non-profit use by private individuals, researchers, and librarians is permitted.

Copyright © 2024 by Gale Richard Walker

All Rights Reserved.

Thirty Questions Regarding the History of Pre-Stockport, Ohio

by

Gale Richard Walker, Ph.D.

ISBN-13: 978-1-7361884-6-0

TURAS Publishing
Life is a Journey

Dedicated to the
Memory of prolific
Muskingum Valley researcher

Clyde K. Swift

Born 1909 in Stockport, Ohio
Died in 1993 in Glen Ellyn, Illinois

The Hills of Old Morgan

The Irish may sing of the Lakes of Killarney,
    And sigh for the land where the Shamrock grows green;
But little I care for the blather and blarney,
    The hills of old Morgan he never has seen.

The longer I'm absent, the more I grow fonder
    Of your emerald hills and your rippling streams—
It matters but little where e'er I may wander,
    Thy scenes and thy beauties steal into my dreams.

I can see the old cabin and the vines that trailed o'er it,
    And the candle that glowed in the window for me;
The home of my childhood, I dearly adore it,
    And a face that has vanished, I'm longing to see.

I can smell honeysuckles and scent the sweet clover,
    Your old fashioned roses my very soul thrills;
When trials and troubles forever are over
    I am coming, fair Morgan, to sleep in thy hills.

                            James Martin Shawhan (1857–1929)
                            — *Unpolished Pebbles,* 1902, p. 115
                            Lowell, Ohio

"My reason teaches me that land cannot be sold. . . . Nothing can be sold, but such things as can be carried away."
— Black Hawk, Sauk Chief (1767-1838)
[quoted in Gale Richard Walker, *The Theft of Ohio*, 2016, p. 531]

"The Indians are generally hated here quite as much as they are pretty well throughout America. But this hate does not always spring from the same reasons, much less from those altogether just. —— It is beginning to be extensively and learnedly posited that none of the Indian tribes, as many of them as are still scattered throughout the whole of broad America, have the remotest right to the land wherein they and their forefathers for unthinkable ages have lived."
— German tourist David Schoepf (1752-1800)
At Pittsburgh, 1783

"Brothers: The commissioners of the United States have formerly set up a claim to your whole country, southward of the great lakes, as the property of the United States, grounding this claim on the treaty of peace [in Paris in 1783] with your father, the King of Great Britain, . . . who declared . . . the middle of those lakes . . . to be the boundaries of the United States. Brothers: We, therefore, frankly tell you, that we think those commissioners put an erroneous construction on that part of our treaty with the King. As he had not purchased the country of you, of course he could not give it away; he only relinquished to the United States his claim to it. . . . Brother: We now concede this great point. We, by the express authority of the President of the United States, acknowledge the property, or right of soil,of the great country above described [the Northwest Territory] to be in the Indian nations, so long as they desire to occupy it."
— U.S. President George Washington conceding, after U.S. General St. Clair's defeat in 1791, via his three U.S. Treaty Commissioners—Benjamin Lincoln, Beverly Randolph, and Timothy Pickering—at British Captain Matthew Elliot's house opposite Detroit, that the entire Northwest Territory rightfully belongs to the native Indian tribes, July 31, 1793.
—[Gale Richard Walker, *The Theft of Ohio*, 2016, p. 615]

Table of Contents

Question Number   **Page**

1. Who Were the First Owners of Stockport Soil? 1
2. Who Were the First European Owners of Pre-Stockport Soil? 3
3. Who Were the First White English-Speaking Owners of Pre-Stockport
    Soil (the western half of R10, T9 Lot #90)? 6
4. Madison or Mathewson Run? 11
5. Who Was the First White Private Individual Owner of Pre-Stockport Soil? 13
6. Who Were the First White English-Speaking Owner-Occupants of
    Pre-Stockport Soil? 20
7. Who Was Kate from Tyler County, Virginia (now West Virginia)? 22
8. Why Did Kate Live at Roxbury, Ohio? 22
9. Where Is Kate Buried? 22
10. What Became of Restless Paddock Cheadle and His Family? 35
11. Who Built the First House on the Future Site of Stockport, Lot #90? 36
12. Who Was the First White Child Born on the Future Site of Stockport? 36
13. Why Have the Names of Rial and Mary (*nee* Tufts) Cheadle's Two
    Daughters Been Kept a Family Secret? 43
14. Who Was the First Person Known to Have Died Near Pre-Stockport Lot #90? . 48
15. Who Was the First White Woman Who Died at the Pre-Stockport Site? 51
16. Who Was the First White Child Born at the Pre-Stockport Site? 52
17. What Became of Pre-Stockport's First Known Native Son, Thomas Cheadle? . 54
18. Who Gave Windsor Township Its Name? 55
19. Who Gave Stockport Its Name? 55
20. Why Has Stockport Survived? The Terrace Theory? 56
21. What Is the Earliest Date on a Tombstone in the Stockport Cemetery? 58
22. What is the Oldest Known Tombstone in Morgan County, Ohio? 58
23. What Is Mother Nott's Hole? 60
24. Where Is Mother Nott's Hole? 60
25. Who Was Mother Nott? 66
26. What Was One of the Most Lamented Tragedies in the Pre-Stockport Era? . . 70
27. Who Described the Tragedy in Both Graphic and Poetic Detail in 1837? . . . 71
28. What Is Now Known Regarding Young Joel Sherman? 75
29 Will I Ever Come to My Final Comments? 76
30. Who Was James B. Johnson of Windsor Township, Morgan County, Ohio? . 80

Appendices

Appendix A
First White Land Owners of Pre-Stockport by Rebecca Faires 84

Appendix B
Record of the Presbyterian Congregation of Windsor [Ohio] 1824-37 85

Appendix C
Stockport as Noted in the Papers, Publications, Manuscripts, and Timelines
by Clyde K. Swift. 88

Appendix D
"Keelboats Crews: A Wondrus Race," by R. E. Banta 91

Appendix E
Who Was Caleb Swan, Jr.? 97

Appendix F
Endubonah. 108

Appendix G
Excerpts from "Nathaniel Evans: A Frontier Soldier," by Elizabeth Cottle . . . 109

Appendix H
"Frederick Eveland of Stockport, Ohio," by Barbara L. Covey. 112

Appendix I
Names and Addresses of Residential Telephone Subscribers in 1993 Listed
Under Stockport, Ohio, Telephone Prefix 614-559-xxxx, 1993 et. al. 123

Appendix J
1950 U.S. Census of Population and Housing, Stockport, Ohio 132

Appendix K
"Old Time Boatmen in 1823" by Clyde K. Swift 149

Question Number 1:

Who Were the First Human Owners of Pre-Stockport Soil?

If one assumes that humans can own land, as virtually all people of European descent now do, then the first owners of the Ohio and Muskingum River valleys, including pre-Stockport soil, were pre-historic northern Asian nomadic people and their descendants. Modern DNA analyses of ancient burial remains of pre-historic Americans repeatedly confirm that the first human inhabitants of North, Central, and South America were all of north Asian ancestry. Specifically, all "native" peoples in the Western Hemisphere, including those who inhabited the Ohio Valley for tens of thousands of years before Christopher Columbus "discovered" what he believed was India—hence misnamed them "Indians"—are descendants of northern Asian ancestors who crossed the ancient land bridge from northeastern Asia (Siberia) and northwestern America (Alaska), now ocean-covered, known as the Bering Strait. Thus, ownership of the Western Hemisphere was theirs by right of first discovery.

Their stone tools, arrowheads, spear points, earthworks, dwellings, villages, cities, carvings, calendars, artworks, remarkable effigies (such as "Serpent Mound" at Peebles, Ohio, and Monks Mound at Cahokia, Illinois), hominy holes, tools, descendants, trails, diverse languages, and thousands of ancestral burial mounds and earth works testify to their industry, antiquity, ubiquity, diversity, crafts, art, cities, and *priority of discovery, occupation, and ownership*.

Many, if not most, of their relics and structures have been destroyed by subsequent European invaders, racists, farmers, thieves, urbanization, collectors, floods, and natural erosion. Only a few small pre-Columbian burial mounds yet survive in Morgan County, Ohio. By 1914 there were less than 40 intact Indian burial mounds remaining in Morgan County, Ohio.[1] And fewer, no doubt, by 2024.

---

[1] *Archaeological Atlas of Ohio*, 1914, pp. 57-8.

The large, circular native American burial mound preserved in Mound Cemetery Marietta, Ohio—Conus Mound—is the largest in the Muskingum watershed. The huge, rectangular, high, flat-topped Cahokia Mound, built for the houses and courts of their rulers and elites, near present-day Cahokia, Illinois, is the largest native earthwork in the United States east of the Mississippi River. There are remnants of even larger ancient cities in South America, some high in the Andes Mountains.

YOUR NOTES

Question Number 2:

Who Were the First European "Owners" of Pre-Stockport Soil?

According to Papal Law of the Holy Roman Empire regarding "first discovery" by a Christian nation, the first owner of the Ohio River and all of the land drained by its tributaries, including the Muskingum River, was France:

> The adventurous La Salle . . . was the first white man who trod the soil of the destined State of Ohio and the first whose eyes beheld the Beautiful river. With a few followers and led by Indian guides he penetrated the vast country of the powerful Iroquois until . . . he reached "a point six or seven leagues from Lake Erie, a branch of the Ohio, which he descended to the main stream," and so went onward as far as the "falls," now the site of Louisville, Kentucky. His men abandoned him there, he retraced his way alone. This . . . was in the winter of 1669-70.

> Prior to the middle of the [18th] century the French strenuously reasserted their ownership of the northwest, and did actually take possession of what is now the northern part of Ohio, building a fort and established a trading station at Sandusky. Celeron de Bienville made a systematic exploration of the Ohio valley and formally declared by process verbal the ownership of the soil. On the sixteenth of August, 1749, he was at the mouth of the Muskingum. This fact was revealed in 1798 by the discovery of a leaden plate which had been buried by him and which set forth that the explorer sent out by the Marquis de la Gallissoniere, captain general of New Grace, agreeable to the wishes of His Majesty, Louis XV, had deposited the plate as a monument of the renewal of possession of *la riviera Oyo*, otherwise la belle riviera, and all those which empty into it, and of all the lands of both sides even to the sources of the said rivers, and which had been obtained by force of arms and by treaties, especially those of Ryswick, Utrecht, and Aix-la-chappell. The plate was found protruding from the bank [at the mouth of the Muskingum] after a freshet, by some boys, who, ignorant of

its antiquarian value, cut away a considerable portion of it to melt into bullets, lead there being very scarce. . . . Considerable difficulty was experienced in making the translation as a portion of the inscription had been cut away by the finders of the plate, but the larger part remaining enabled [William Woodbridge at Marietta, who had been studying French at Gallipolis] to supply the missing words. The plate was nearly twelve inches from top to bottom and about seven and a half in breadth. A similar plate was found in 1846 at the mouth of the Kanawha. They were doubtless deposited at the mouths of all the principal tributaries of the Ohio.[2]

French, Dutch, and German missionaries, agents, ambassadors, and armies were by far the most morally astute Europeans to invade North America. Indeed, unlike others with respect to the Ohio Valley, French Catholics and the French government took it for granted that North America rightfully belonged to the various indigenous, polyglot cultures they found living there. Unlike others, the French had little, if any, aversion to adopting Indian customs, marrying Indian women, and sharing in their customs and fortunes. The early history of Vincennes, Indiana, serves as a typical case in the Ohio River watershed. French Catholics built and dedicated a church at Vincennes two years before George Washington was born! Indeed, the first Europeans to see the Ohio River were French explorers and traders travelling up it—southwest-to-northeast—not down it. Eventually, however, the British gained and claimed possession from the French via the French and Indian War, then General George Washington and Anglo-Americans gained possession of the Ohio Valley from the British via the Revolutionary War.

There was one positive aspect in all that self-serving and self-righteous prejudice, warfare, conquest, greed, slavery, theft, cruelty, religious piety, and racism. To wit, the native inhabitants of the Ohio River Valley, unlike major parts of Central and South America, seldom suffered the grotesque, gruesome, and ghastly

---

[2] H. Z. Williams, *History of Washington County, Ohio, 1788-1881*, pp. 16-7. (1881, reprinted 1976)

inhumanities inflicted under Spanish Catholic rule. Spanish priests took native women for their own purposes and enslaved the men, working them to death on plantations in North, Central, and South America and in silver and gold mines. Although Christopher Columbus eventually died in chains in a prison in Valladolid, Spain, on May 20, 1506, subsequent Spanish explorers and exploiters soon made Spain the richest country in Europe.

YOUR NOTES

Question Number 3:

Who Were the First White English-Speaking Owners of Pre-Stockport Soil (i.e., the western half of R10, T9, Lot #90)?

The first official white private land owner in the United States of the future site of Stockport was not an individual, but a post-Revolutionary War land development corporation headquartered in Massachusetts—The Ohio Company—which began its onsite possession and operations at the mouth of the Muskingum River on April 7, 1788. The Company purchased the land from the U.S. Government, which had acquired it via three extorted post-Revolutionary War U.S.-Indian treaties—at Fort Stanwix in New York in 1784; Fort McIntosh (Beaver, Pennsylvania, 25 miles down the Ohio River from Fort Pitt) in 1785; and Fort Finney (near the future site of Cincinnati) in 1786.

Those three extorted treaties—which fomented cruelty, vengeance, turmoil, and war instead of peace on the Ohio frontier—forced Treaty Commissioner/Northwest Territorial Governor Arthur St. Clair to repeat U.S. threats of war and annihilation at the two-treaties-in-one, which he held at Fort Harmar on the Muskingum in 1788-89. "If you want war, you shall have war," Arthur St. Clair threatened the Ohio Valley and Northwestern chiefs assembled at Fort Harmar at Marietta, Ohio—which triggered seven more years of U.S. Army versus Indian Confederation Army warfare in the Northwest Territory.

After the Indian Confederation defeated the U.S. Army led by General Harmar in 1790, then defeated the U.S. Army led by General/Governor Arthur St. Clair in 1791, President Washington dropped his long-running pretense of past U.S. purchases at extorted treaties and formally admitted in 1793 that all prior U.S. treaties with the various tribes (at Forts Stanwix, McIntosh, Finney, and Harmar) had been extorted. No free sales or purchases—as explicitly required by U.S. law in the Land Ordinance of 1787—had occurred. President Washington's "great concession," delivered to the chiefs by U.S. treaty commissioner Timothy Pickering, et. al., at British Captain Matthew Elliot's house opposite Detroit on July 31, 1793:

> Brother: We now concede this great point. We, by the express authority of the President of the United States, acknowledge the property, or right of soil, of the great country above described [the entire Northwest Territory] to be in the Indian nations, so long as they desire to occupy it.[3]

Ohio Company CEO Rufus Putnam at Marietta, who admitted he had known the truth all along—*even before he arrived in Ohio on April 7, 1788, to sell, grant, and give the Indians' lands in Ohio to whites*—likewise admitted the theft of Ohio and explicitly (albeit belatedly) said so in writing, including in his correspondence to President Washington. At all former treaties the land had been, in Putnam's own words, "wrested from them," not freely purchased as required by U.S. law. The proof is both simple and startling: Read the dialogue at each of the four U.S. treaty locations cited above. To wit, after seven years of Revolutionary War, the new American negotiators, intoxicated by their victory over the army and navy of the British Empire, arrogantly, repeatedly, and legally incriminated themselves in writing—*as conquerors, not purchasers*—at all four of the treaty sites cited above, in blatant, systematic, and irrefutable violation of the U.S. Ordinance of 1787, which explicitly required the free sale and purchase of all Indian land.

But after General Anthony Wayne's troops defeated the confederated Indian tribes at Fallen Timbers on the Maumee River in 1794, all of that—including Washington's "great concession"—was swept under the rug of greed, racism, and revisionist U.S. history. The Ohio Company then hired young, energetic Israel Ludlow to help finish the survey of the Ohio Company's large, odd-shaped perimeter.

---

[3] Gale Richard Walker, *Theft of Ohio, 1783-1795*, 2016, p. 615.

Today (2024) the Ohio Company's final northern border, known as the Ludlow Line, passes east-to-west 1.1 miles due south of Morgan High School. In fact, all of the long, straight part of the northern border of present-day Windsor Township in Morgan County is a portion of Ludlow's long survey line from the Ohio River due west. And east of Windsor Township, it is now also the boundary between the south border of Center Township, Morgan County, and the north border of Washington County.

Would you like to drive on it? When driving south from McConnelsville to Stockport on SR376, beginning a few chains east of its junction with Taylor Hollow Road (TR214), the straight due-east stretch of SR376, one-quarter mile long, is a segment of Israel Ludlow's original east-west northern boundary of what years later became the Ohio Company's northern boundary.

Where did Ludlow begin his due-west line? Ludlow had been hired to survey a line due west from the southernmost point where one of the north-south range lines of the Seven Ranges in easternmost Ohio had struck the Ohio River in 1785 (three years before the Ohio Company arrived at the Muskingum). Today that point is near Fly, Ohio. He surveyed that due-west line in May and June, 1789.

Once Ludlow and other survey crews finished surveying the perimeter of the Ohio Company Purchase, setting posts six miles apart, additional survey crews were hired to crisscross its interior with Range (north-south) and Township (east-west) lines, then subdivide them by gridding them into either 36 one-square mile sections (numbered 1 to 36) or into long narrow, rectangular "lots" for special purposes, such as maximizing the access to rivers and river bottom land. Some Lots contained 100 acres, others 160, etc.

For example, the Ohio Company hired Jeffery Mathewson (1761-1833) of Liston, Connecticut, to survey much of what eventually became Windsor Township, Morgan County, Ohio. One entry in his field notes in April, 1796, is of special interest. While surveying *due south* from an Ohio Company stake on the Ludlow Line (which a perimeter crew had previously set west of the Muskingum about a mile due west of present-day Hooksburg), Mathewson, while setting the corner posts of adjacent lots, noted a natural spring near the west-end of pre-Stockport. Matthewson's field notes in Range 11, Township 9, surveying due south in 1796:

> 3d Mile S[outh from the stake of origin on Ludlow's east-west perimeter Line, I] Continued — Running between the Hill & Bottom [i.e., along the west bank of a ridge running north-south. At] 28.79 chains [0.74 miles from last corner post] [I] Set a Post [at the west corner of Lots] No. 90 & 91 . . . a large spring rises at the foot of the hill about 80 l[in]ks [52.8 ft.] NW from this Post and runs an easterly course a stream 10 links [6.5 ft.] wide. [4] [5]

A few decades later, no doubt to be near that freshwater spring, pre-Stockport settlers built a one-room schoolhouse in the west end of Lot #90. Although when, where, who, names of teachers and students, the school's features, terms, duration, cost, demise, etc., are unknown, "Big Spring," as it is known locally, continues to discharge fresh water, sending it south across SR266, to meander down Turkey Run southeastward to the Muskingum River at the south edge of Stockport near the foot of Salt Works Hill. Specifically, Big Spring is located

---

[4] Ohio Company Surveyor Records, *Mathewson's Notebook* #1, April, 1796, p. 9, Marietta College Archives, Marietta, Ohio. His descriptions of bearing trees for each corner post are omitted. See the Ohio Company survey map on page 18.

[5] For the record: Mathewson's survey notes as he continued due south from the west end of pre-Stockport: "33.30 chs. [chains] a Stream 15 lks. [links] wide Runs E. 40. [chs.] Set a Post No. 1060 & 1061. ... 41.90 [chains south] On a thick brush side hill Set a Post [at the corner of Lots] No. 91 & 92 .... 51.40 [chains south] On Oak Hill Lane to a small stream Runs E. .... 55.1 [chains south] Set a Post No. 92 & 93 .... 60. [chains south] Set a Post [at the corner of Lots] No. 1061 & 1062 .... 69 [chains south] set a Post No. 93 & 94 .... 01. The Township line Set a Post at the Intersection for the Corners of 100 acre lot No. 94 and 160 Acre lot No. 1062 in this Township and for 160 [-acre] lots No. 1109 & 1129 in the 8th Township. .... The Hill Land in this Mile is Principally Timbered with Oak and thick with Brush. [End of p. 9]" His routine descriptions of "bearing trees" and the distance of each to its respective corner post are omitted since both are long gone.

northwest of the west corporation limit sign at Stockport, on the *north* side of SR266, behind and near the house of the late Harold "Heck" Harkins [1921–2004] family.[6]

On October 27, 1798, two years after Mathewson's survey, quoted above:

> The first mail route [was] established within the present limits of Ohio. Daniel Converse [1775-1848], an early pioneer who came with his family to Marietta in 1788, came to the Beverly-Waterford Settlement in 1789 and was hired as the first mail contractor.[7] The schedule required that the post should leave Marietta [by water] every Thursday at 1:00 p.m. and arrive at Zanesville the following Monday at 8:00 a.m. The return trip started from Zanesville [by water] every Tuesday at 6:00 a.m. arriving in Marietta on Wednesday at 6:00 p.m.
>
> This route was discontinued in 1804. By the year 1825, the mail was carried [on horseback] from Marietta to Zanesville once a week.[8] In December 1867 it went "From Pennsville, by Stockport, Roxbury, and Brown's Mills, to Watertown, 17 3/4 miles and back once a week."

---

[6] Long-time Morgan County Engineer Stevan Hook, originally from Stockport, is an authority on the topic of Big Spring at Stockport as well as the tools, methods and maps of early chain-carrying surveyors.

[7] Convers' mail contract is dated October 27, 1798. The three-page contract is shown in Walker, *Stockport, Ohio*, pp. 32 a-c. Daniel Convers had previously been held captive by the Ottawa and Chippewa: "In April 1791, Converse, a young man . .. , was at work with some companions in the woods a short distance from Fort Frye, when a party of nine Ottawa and Chippewa Indians rose up from behind a brush fence and fired upon them. His companions fled to the garrison and Converse, left alone was taken prisoner and carried away to Sandusky, and from there to Detroit. The period of his captivity was only about six weeks. He passed through varied experiences, was treated for the most part very kindly, and finally made his escape and worked his way slowly eastward from one British post to another until he reached the American settlements, and then journeyed through to his home at Killingly, Connecticut, where he remained until 1794, when he again ventured to the west and located at Marietta." (H.Z. Williams, *History of Washington County, Ohio*, 1881, p. 78)

[8] Winnie (*nee* Smith) Johnson, *That's Where It All Began*, 1988, pp. 36-8. "Beverly/Waterford Bicentennial [Celebration], 1789-1989."

Question Number 4:

Madison or Mathewson Run?

Madison Run empties into the Muskingum near tiny Brokaw, originally known as Shacksville, which, at one time or another, hosted a general store, grade school, post office, ferry, stone quarry, and, beginning on May 15, 1897, a flag-stop on the Zanesville & Ohio Railroad.[9] In 1908 C. W. Thornily and Arley Johnson purchased J. W. Leake's store at Brokaw. Today there are only a few houses in the vicinity.

In 1958 Marietta historian George Blazier suggested that "Madison Run" is actually a misperception of the sound of "Mathewson," the man who first surveyed most of that region.[10] Furthermore, there never has been anyone named Madison associated with that or any other part of the lower Muskingum in pioneer times. Ohio Company records at Marietta College indicate that the only other Ohio Company surveyors with compass and chain who initially criss-crossed Range 11 Township 9 in the late 1790s and early 1800s were Return Jonathan Meigs, Jonathan Stone, and Anselm Tupper.

Irene Evans (1904-1984), in her notes in 1964 on farm life growing up near Brokaw (now [2024] the Richard and Susan Barrett properties between Roxbury and Brokaw) included her hand-drawn early Ohio Company Lot, Section, Township, and Range lines, who owned which parcels, when purchased, from whom, price, etc. Interestingly, along "Madison Run", flowing north to the river at Brokaw, she penciled in the words, "Matthewson Run."[11] "Madison" may, indeed, have been an Ohio Company mapmaker's misperception of the sound of "Mathewson."

---

[9] *Marietta Daily Leader*, May 15, 1897. The railroad from Zanesville via Marietta to Parkersburg, West Virginia, was originally the Black Diamond R.R., then the Ohio & Little Kanawha R.R., then the Zanesville & Ohio R.R., and finally the Baltimore & Ohio R.R.
[10] George J. Blazier, ed., *Joseph Barker, Recollections of the First Settlement of Ohio*, 1958, p. 39ff.
[11] Ms. Irene Evans, on her maps and in her notes, drafted circa 1964, regarding the first school at Shacksville, later known as Brokaw, wrote: (Footnote 11 continued at the bottom of next page)

Who is unknown. Imagine that you were Mathewson! After all of your difficult work with compass and chain, trekking over steep hills, down ravines, and across a crooked river and winding creeks and thick bogs, contending with briars, thorns, copperheads, bears, bobcats, skunks, wasps, hornets, wind, rain, heat, lightning, thieves, and wolves[12]—after all of that—a mapmaker then misapprehends, thus misspells your last name on a little run on official maps, misnaming you for all posterity!

YOUR NOTES

[Footnote 11 continued from page 11]: "Dec. 13, 1838 (notarized), Wm. T. Evans leased part of #37 to Directors of School Dist. #6, Roxbury Twp., for as long as [it remains] occupied by [a] school. (On E. Bank of 'Materson' [sic] Run, 80 Rods from mouth.) Jan. 1, 1839. It was afterwards called Brokaw School, after the Post Office, which was named for Geo. Brokaw, who was the 1st postmaster" [Irene Evans' notes courtesy of Richard Martin and Chester Cunningham].

Walker: Older residents of Stockport remember Billy Wootton (1872-1964) as a dry-goods merchant at Stockport. However, as a young man, Billy taught a few terms at Brokaw School, walking five miles from Stockport to Brokaw and back every school day. In 1913 teacher Ford Ball was headmaster of students Helen Ball, Tilman ("Doc") Kenney, Glen Evans, Jewel White, Kenneth Ball, Julia Kinney, Mabel and Maude Thorniley, Lucille White, Louise Leake, Lizzie Dyke, Edith Evans, Lew Evans, Dayton Hoover, Ralph Johnson, Irene Evans, Cecil Hoover, Robert Kinney, Hugh Robinson, Doris Walker, Goldie Thorniley, Louanna Walker, Stella Lane, Herb Robinson, Beeman Kinney, and Ted Ball. At least six of the 26 students, according to the late Grace (*nee* Kirkbride) Walker (1912-2008) of Stockport, became school teachers: Julia Kinney, Lucille White, Edith Evans, Robert Kinney, Stella Lane, and Herb Robinson. (See also the masterful booklet by the late Raymond Oliver, *School Memories, Morgan County,* Vol. I, April 1991, "Shacksville Grade School 1913, Later Known as BROKAW," p. 31.)

[12] In 1830 in the lower Muskingum Valley: "Wolves still being killed for bounty. Bears are gone." (Clyde K. Swift, *Muskingum Years*, 1980). "Wolves were numerous and very troublesome to the early settlers. Although no instances are remembered of their attacks upon people, many an aged pioneer can recall the time when stock (especially sheep) was often attacked and killed by them. The last wolves in this region, according to the recollection of J. P. Dearborn, were killed in 1832, by Levi Allen of Waterford." (Charles Robertson, *History of Morgan County, Ohio,* 1886, p. 394.)

Question Number 5:

Who Was the First White Private Individual Owner of Pre-Stockport Soil?

The first official white U.S. citizen landowner of the future site of Stockport was U.S. Army Paymaster Caleb Swan, Jr. (7/2/1758–11/29/1809), a post he held for 16 years (1792–1808). He was a Revolutionary War veteran from Massachusetts. Caleb Swan, Jr.'s father and mother were Caleb Swan, Sr., and Dorothy (*nee*) Frye Swan (1731–1821). They also had a daughter whom they named Dorothy Swan. Caleb Swan, Jr.'s, sister Dorothy, married Nathaniel Frye. They had son Nathaniel Frye, Jr., the nephew to whom Caleb Swan, Jr. will later give land in his will.

Dorothy, Sr., who wed Caleb Swan, Sr., was a first cousin of Capt. Joseph Frye (1743–1828), who wed Mary Robinson, thus was an aunt of Joseph and Mary's son, Lieut. Joseph Frye (1765–1814) of Beverly, for whom Fort Frye was later named. The late, excellent historian Phillip Crane (1948-2020) at the Lower Muskingum Historical Society at Beverly, Ohio, outlined part of the relationship between the Swan and Frye families at Fort Frye in frontier days.[13]

Gen. 1: John Frye, (1672-1737), Lieut., wed (11/1/1694) Tabitha Farnum (1678-1755). They had 13 children, which included sons Isaac and Joseph:
    Gen. 2: Isaac Frye (1699-1741) wed Hannah Haskell (1699-1741)
        Gen. 3: Dorothy Frye (1731-1821) wed Caleb Swan, Sr. (1758-1809)
            Gen. 4: Caleb Swan, Jr. (1758-1809) (owner of Lot #90)
    Gen. 2: Joseph Frye, I (1712-1794), Maj. Gen.
        Gen. 3: Joseph Frye, II (1743-1828), Capt., wed Mary Robinson
            Gen. 4: Joseph Frye, III (1765-1814), Lieut. [of Fort Frye fame]
Ergo: **Gen. 3**: Dorothy Frye and Joseph Frye, Capt., were **first** cousins.
4th Gen: Caleb Swan, Jr., and Lieut. Joseph Frye, III, for whom the fort at Beverly was named, were **second** cousins.[14]

---

[13][14] See *Reflections Along the Muskingum*, "Lt. Joseph Frye, His Namesake, Fort Frye, and His Family," Part 1A, Vol. 36, No. 2, April-June, 2010, and Part 1B, Vol. 37, No. 2, April-May-June, 2011, pp. 6-9.

During his official trips to the Northwest Territory, Caleb Swan, Jr., no doubt visited kin and friends at Waterford, but how often is not known.[15] Late in life, Swan willed a city block in Cincinnati, as well as 77.5 acres outside of the city, to his nephew, Nathaniel Frye, Jr., son of Capt./Maj. Nathaniel Frye, Sr. (1753-1833), who was one of 11 children of Major General Joseph Frye (1712-1794) and Mehitabel (*nee*) Poore (1714-1788).[16] Swan's will: ". . . [to] Nathaniel Frye, junr my nephew." Said again, Maj. Nathaniel Frye, Sr.'s, wife was Dorothy *nee* Swan (1752-1847), Caleb Swan, Jr.'s, sister; thus Nathaniel was their nephew.[17]

Although Caleb Swan, Jr., did not live in the Muskingum Valley, he owned one share of Ohio Company stock. When the Ohio Company distributed its final land assets to shareholders in 1796, Swan's one share entitled him to a total of 1,173 acres of Ohio Company land, scattered here and there. Per Ohio Company records, of the seven land parcels of different shapes, sizes, and places to which Swan was entitled, his 100-acre lot, likely allocated by the luck of the draw, was Lot #90 in Range 11, Township 9, Section 25—pre-Stockport.[18]

Lot #90 is a long, narrow, east-west rectangle spanning the Muskingum—about half on each side of the river—in the northernmost part of the Ohio Company Purchase. The lot includes the rich, flat bottoms on the east side of the river (the late John and Chet Porter farms) and the large hill east of them; and west from the river's west bank, Lot #90 includes a steep incline that quickly lessens to a gently rising terrace, the vast majority of which is immune to the river's raging floods and ravaging ice jams—a good place for a settlement. (See pp. 17-18.)

---

[15] See the late Phillip Crane's remarkable gift to future Muskingum Valley generations: *Index to Reflections Along the Muskingum,* Vol. I, 2014, 780 pp., about 20,000 names, and 2,000 pictures!
[16] A major data source of Frye genealogy is Charlotte Helen Abbott's work at Family Search.
[17] N.B., Nathaniel Frye's wife, Dorothy Swan, was "Jr." i.e., a daughter of Dorothy Frye, "Sr." (1731-1821). Caleb Swan, Jr., willed his properties at and near Cincinnati to Nathaniel Frye, Sr.'s (1753-1833) son, Nathaniel Frye, Jr. (1779-1856). Appreciation is due my wife Lori (*nee* Beaver) for *trying* to help me unscramble the complex Swan-Frye genealogy. Also see Ellen Frye Barker, *Frye Genealogy*, 1920, pp. 50, 53-56, and 66. Also see Appendix E herein.
[18] Ohio Company Records, Marietta College, Marietta, Ohio.

Swan's 100-acre Lot #90 at pre-Stockport was incidental to his overall wealth. In 1801 he owned a major part of a 4,000-acre tract, pooled from veterans' land warrants, located just east of Coshocton in the U.S. Military District, a region more or less between Zanesville and Millersburg, which the U.S. government set aside in 1796 to be given to Revolutionary War veterans in parcels based on their military rank. Foot soldiers received 100 acres; ensigns, 150; lieutenants, 200; captains, 300; majors, 400; colonels, 500; on up the ranks to major generals, each of whom received 1,100 acres.

By U.S. law—that is, as rigged by rich Easterners—most acreage in Ohio was sold in New York City to wealthy land speculators whose agents were forced to aggregate small parcels into huge pools of thousands of acres before any legal settlement could begin.[19] Since small land grants were thereby rendered of little practical value to the vast majority of war veterans, they sold their scrip (deeds/warrants/titles) to western land jobbers and eastern real estate brokers. Thus, the vast majority of soldiers got virtually nothing for the small parcels Congress had granted them. What Swan thought of this legal racket and abuse of the poorest soldiers, he did not say. Rather, Swan—a military officer in the U.S. capital—was one of the eager wheeler-dealer speculators in thousands of acres in Ohio.

In late 1795 or early 1796 Swan sold his Muskingum Lot #90 to Major Thomas Doyle of Cincinnati—price, pomp, and circumstances unknown.[20] Swan died in 1809 and was buried in Old Presbyterian Cemetery in Washington, D.C. However, in a ceremony held 83 years later—May 12, 1892—Swan's remains, along with the remains of two other Revolutionary War soldiers, William W. Burrows and General James House, were exhumed and reinterred in Arlington National Cemetery. A stone slab now identifies Swan's grave, located in Section 1-301-C.

---

[19] James Petro, Ohio Land: *A Short History*, Office of the Auditor of State, 1997, pp. 28-9.
[20] A chronology of the legal owners of Lot #90 is given in Appendix A.

Caleb Swan, Jr., Age 41 in 1799

FIRST U.S. CITIZEN TO OWN

PRE-STOCKPORT SOIL

(Range 11, Township 9; Section 25; Lot #90)

* * *   * * *   * * *

TABLE ONE

The Four Boundaries of the Portion of Lot #90 West of the Muskingum River

Northern Border (east-west line): Per Google Earth in 2022, a segment of Lot #90's northern border now manifests in Stockport as short Elmwood Street. Thus, extending that line due east to the river and due west (across Tieber Road, across the RV park, and up the hillside into the woods several rods to intersect Mathewson's north-south survey line) completes the north border and fixes Lot #90's northwest corner first established in 1796. (Thus, technically speaking, all of the houses in Stockport north of the center of Elmwood Street are in Lot #89, north of the original town plat).

Eastern Border (north-south line): Assumed to be the west bank of the Muskingum River.

Southern Border (east-west line): The north edge of Broadway Street from the river due west to the corporation limit sign (where Main Street and Broadway Street merge). (G. W. Sanborn added an addition, now Market St., south from Broadway St. called "Stockport" in 1839.)

Western Border (south to north): An imaginary line from near the west corporation limit sign due north to the northwest corner post of Lot #90 on the hillside in the woods first set by Mathewson in April 1796. (See map on page 18.)

The Boundaries of the Plat of the Town of Windsor in 1834[21]

The village of Windsor (now Stockport) would not be legally platted until 38 years after Jeffrey Mathewson's survey in 1796—specifically, by landowner Nathan Sidwell, Jr., dated May 1, 1834. The initial town plat was only 20 acres of Sidwell's farm, all in the half of Lot #90 west of the river. The sites of the initial house lots to be sold flanked three streets: North Street on the north, Broadway Street (SR266) on the south, with Main Street down the middle between them—in all, six rows of lots facing three streets. Both the town and township populations grew steadily for the next 100 years. Sixteen years later—1850—Windsor Township had the largest population (1,592) of any township in Morgan County. Stockport grew from 118 in 1840, to 289 in 1870, to a peak of 558 in 1980. But due to economic shifts or closures of area industries in recent decades, its population has declined: 1990 pop. 462; 2000 pop. 540; 2010 pop. 503; 2020 pop. 483.

---

[21] Morgan County, Ohio, Judge James Madison Gaylord (1811-1874) states, "Coming down to 1832, we find that Nathan Sidwell, Jr., laid out on the west bank of the river the village of Windsor; in 1833, the Beswicks and Joseph McMahan laid out an addition, and in 1839 G. W. Sanburn [sic] laid out an adjoining village, and named it Stockport, and from appearance it is one village. (James Gaylord, *Historical Reminiscences of Morgan County*, c.1882-3, pp. 60-1). Reprinted from *The Weekly Herald*, McConnelsville, Ohio, 1932, and reprinted by the Morgan County Historical Society in McConnelsville, Ohio, in April 1964. Herein 1834 is used. See Appendix A.

North-to-South survey line west of the Muskingum River down which Jeffery Mathewson surveyed in April, 1796—setting Lot corner posts, citing bearing trees, land quality, springs, notable features, etc.

Partial view of Ohio Company Range XI, Township IX map. Surveyor Jeffery Mathewson set the west corner post of Lots #90/#91 in April, 1796. The * in the northeast corner of Lot #1060, slightly northwest of the corner post may be near the site of the Big Spring. The long creek southeast to the river is Bald Eagle, 6.4 miles long. The future site of Stockport, 40 years later, is the western half of Lot #90, bottom center. Hooksburg (not shown) is on Lot #76 (top) east of the river. (Ohio Company Map Collection, Marietta College, Marietta, Oh.)

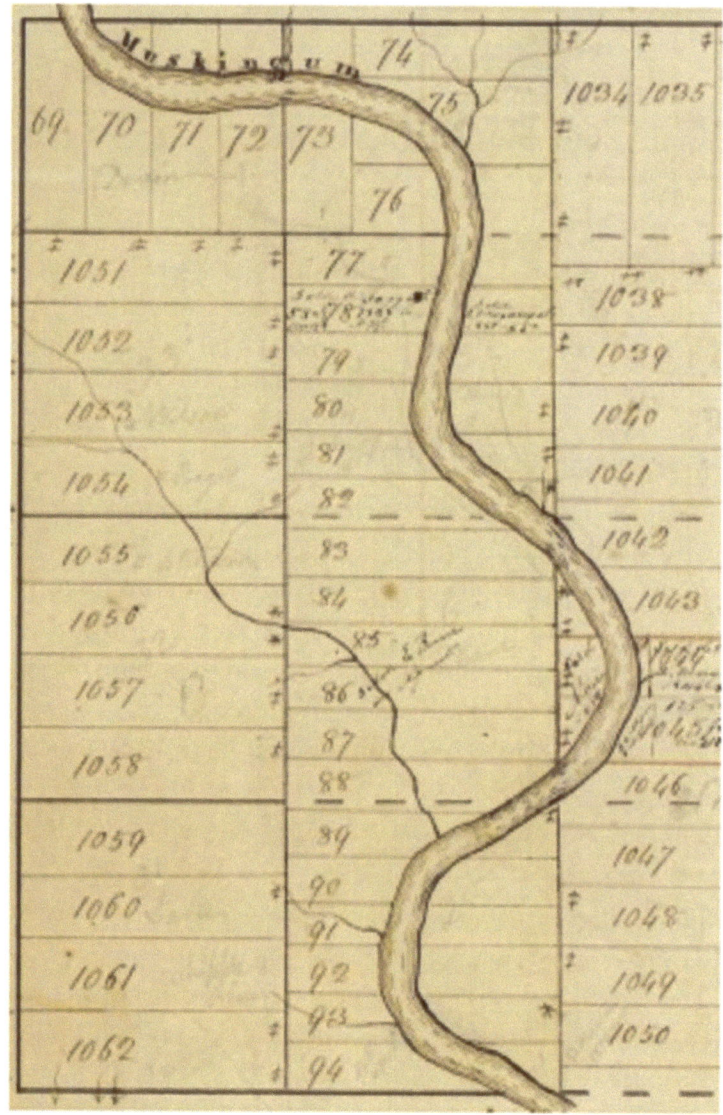

* * * * * * * * *

In review, the first white owner of the long, narrow lot through which Main Street in Stockport (west-to-east) gently rises, then gently slopes, then drops to the river, was a Revolutionary War veteran, a clerk in the office of U.S. Secretary of War Henry Knox, a U.S. Indian agent to the Creek Indians, Paymaster of the U.S. Army appointed by President Washington, a signatory of the U.S.-Indian Treaty of Greeneville in 1795, a slave owner, an author and authority on Creek Indian culture, owner of hundreds of bounty land acreage in Ohio near

Coshocton, Zanesville, and in and near Cincinnati, and one of only eleven Revolutionary War soldiers buried in Arlington National Cemetery.

Whether paymaster Swan ever saw his Ohio Company Lot #90 is not known, but given his friends and close relatives at Waterford and Fort Frye (Beverly) and his frequent journeys crisscrossing the Northwest Territory, he likely passed up and down the Muskingum River on occasion. If so, he poled and/or drifted across the 100-acre lot which would become, by virtue of his one share in the Ohio Company, one of his many and much larger properties.[22]

YOUR NOTES

---

[22]"Lieutenant Joseph Frye, the designer of Fort Frye, has many descendants, but no living male descendants with the name Frye. Of course the Frye name is fairly common, but none are living male descendants of Lt. Joseph Frye. As far as can be determined, the Fort Frye Local School District and Fort Frye High School are his namesakes that have the best chance to carry on his surname. The male members of Lt. Joseph Frye's family in America fit into three occupation types. The first known generations were prominent military men. The next two generations were mainly farmers. The more recent generations were college educated, producing a civil engineer and a geologist. Starting with Lt. Joseph Frye's progeny, there was only one male descendant in each generation who produced a male offspring. With such a small number with the Frye name, it was only a matter of time before the male descendants of Lt. Joseph Frye with his surname died out." [The article continues for three more pages.] Excerpted from "**Lt. Frye's male namesakes dead**," by Phill Crane, *The Marietta Times*, December 21, 2013, pp. 1-4.

Question Number 6:

Who Was the First White English-Speaking Owner-Occupants of Pre-Stockport Soil?

According to the notes, records, and reminiscences of Morgan County Judge James M. Gaylord (1811-1874) of McConnelsville, Ohio, written circa 1872-73:

Windsor Township was organized like the other new townships of the county. The county commissioners set it off by bounds, and the court, at their July term, and on the 7th day of July, 1819, made the following order in regard to this township:

"Whereas, it appears to the court that our commissioners of Morgan county have erected a new township by the name of Windsor; ordered, that the township be entitled to two justices of the peace, and that the qualified electors of said township be authorized to assemble at the house of John Lucas in said township, on Saturday, the 24th instant, for the purpose of electing two justices of the peace for said township of Windsor."

In compliance with the above order the pioneer voters of the township met on the 24th day of July, 1819, and organized themselves into a town meeting and proceeded with the election. The first thing they did was to appoint Richard Cheadle, Silvanus Newton and Silvanus Olney, judges, and Ephraim Wight and Samuel M. Dike the clerks to conduct the election.

The number of pioneers turning out and voting at this election numbered 44, and is believed to be a full list of the adult males of the township: . . . The early pioneer settlers [in alphabetical order]:

John Cheadle, John Cheadle, Jr.; Joseph Cheadle, Padock (sic) Cheadle, Richard Cheadle, Brazilla Coburn, Nicholas Coburn, John Craft, Levi Davis, Thomas Davis,

Wm. Davis, 1st; Wm. Davis, Luther Dearborn, Nathan Dearborn, Daniel Dennis, 2nd; Samuel Dennis, Michael Devin, Samuel M. Dike, Alfred Ellis, Ephraim Ellis, Ephraim Ellis (sic), Levi Ellis, Asa Emerson, Jr.; David Emerson, Frederick Eveland, Nathaniel Eveland, Prince Godfrey, Elisha Hand, Samuel Henry, Wm. Henry, Franklin Hersey, Samuel Johnson, Nathaniel Lucas, Isaac Melvin, John Methany, Joseph Morris, Silvanus Newton, Silvanus Olney, Lyman Sherman, Samuel Stacy, Barney Sutliff, Adelphia Webster, Joseph Widger, Ephraim Wight.

At this election, Isaac Melvin received 29 votes, Adelphia Webster 39, Levi Ellis 14, Samuel White, Richard Cheadle and Ephraim Wight one vote each. Melvin and Webster were by the usual proclamation declared the expounders of law and the dispensers of justice for the next three years within the bailiwick of the new township of Windsor.[23]

About 1821 young Paddock Cheadle of Big Bottom bought 112 acres of the future site of Stockport (near where the high school stood and the cemetery is now) from Luther Dearborn for $200, then sold half of it to a relative, Joseph Cheadle, later that year. What is known regarding this young, free-spirited, muscular fellow, Paddock (a.k.a. Paddick) Cheadle?

YOUR NOTES

---

[23] James M. Gaylord, *Historical Reminiscences of Morgan County*, 1882-83, pp. 57-8. Reprinted from *The Weekly Herald*, McConnelsville, Ohio, 1932, and reprinted by the Morgan County Historical/Genealogical Society (OGS Chapter #59), April 1984.

Questions Number 7, Number 8, and Number 9:

Who Was Kate from Tyler County, Virginia (now West Virginia)?
Why Did Kate Live at Roxbury, Ohio? Where Is Kate Buried?

Whereas slave-owner Caleb Swan never lived in what is now Morgan County, Ohio, another slave owner did and—believe it or not—the slave's owner was a woman, Rachel (*nee* Ankrum) Cheadle, who, with her new husband Paddock Cheadle, lived at Big Bottom on Lot #100 (now part of the Michael Porter farm), next to his brother, John Cheadle, who lived on what, decades later, became John Buck's (1846–1921) farm—to future generations simply "the Buck Farm."[24][25]

On early maps of southeastern Ohio—such as Ohio Company Township and Range line survey maps, Henry Carey's Map of Ohio in 1814, maps of the Muskingum River, etc.—only one European settlement is shown in what is now Morgan County: Roxbury. The only other area settlements shown are Waterford, Ames (now Amesville in Athens County), and Worster (aka Wooster) but known as Watertown after 1824 (now in Washington County, Ohio).

---

[24] The distance from the bridge at Stockport, Ohio, down-river to the sharp right-angle bend in SR266, where the Buck Farm house yet stood as late as the 1960s, but is now gone, is 2.6 miles. [Google Earth]

[25] "John Buck was born in Virginia on March 18, 1799. His father Anthony Buck was born in Ireland. In 1801 the family moved to Washington County, PA. John drove a stage on the National Turnpike, then built culverts and bridges on that road, in partnership with Truxton Lyon. In 1836 Buck and Lyon (the latter became a state representative to the Ohio Legislature in 1841) and Christian Wolf were awarded contracts to build two locks and part of a canal at Taylorsville, one lock and dam at Luke Chute, one lock and dam at Waterford, and two locks and part of a canal at Lowell. In 1840 Buck and Lyon bought over $8,000 of land on the north side of the Muskingum at Luke Chute and above, at and adjoining the ill-fated town of Big Rock platted by Asa Emerson [See Question #20 below]. Lyon sold out to John Buck in 1848. The Buck Farm was a Big Bottom landmark. John Buck, Jr., and his son Charles farmed there. John Buck, Sr., married Jane Wier in 1828 in Pennsylvania and had three children: Thomas, Samuel W., and Margaret. Mrs. Buck died on October 13, 1834. In 1839 John Buck, Sr., then married Esther Hunter in Westmoreland, PA, and had Jane (who wed a man named Tucker), Hettie (who wed a Muse), and John Buck, Jr. John Buck, Sr., died February 24, 1877. In 1787 Charles R. Buck, a son of John, Jr., along with James R Martin, bought and ran the steamboat "L. C. McCormick." She sank in 1879. They then built the "Gen'l H.F. Devol." (Clyde K. Swift, *Men on the Muskingum*, 1971).

Roxbury—shown on early maps as "Frisbey's Landing"—was an early warehouse, ferry, and shipping port in Roxbury Township (formed in 1806) in Washington County. It was annexed into Morgan County in 1851. In fact, Roxbury Township's boundary was changed in 1806, 1807, 1810, 1811, 1814, 1817, 1831, 1845, 1846, then dissolved in 1851—too tedious to log here.[26] For example, due to such shifting political boundaries, one early farmer near Bartlett lived in three different counties (Washington, Athens, Morgan) and never moved; likewise, a few farmers on Lightner Ridge west of Stockport such as John Walker (1842-1903). His uncle Alexander, a veteran of the War of 1812, was granted bounty land (in Washington County); John built a brick house on it in another county (Morgan), then married in a third county (Athens)—all at the same site.

On February 27, 1845, the Marietta *Intelligencer* noted a bill was introduced in the Ohio Legislature "to attach Sections 5, 6, 12, 29, 35, and 36 in Roxbury Township, Washington County [along river] to Morgan County."[27] As well, in January 1846, 21 citizens of Sections No. 1, 2, 3, and 4 of Roxbury Township, Washington County, petitioned the Ohio Legislature to attach them to Morgan County.[28] It did. The remainder of Roxbury Township became part of Palmer Township in Washington County. Of the 25 townships originally comprising Washington County, Ohio, only two ceased to exist—Roxbury and Jolly.

As noted, square-mile sections along the Muskingum (like those at Big Bottom and pre-Stockport) were subdivided into rectangles, often 100-acres each, often spanning the river, thus providing more lots with rich, level, river-bottom soil as well as river access to markets, thus attract more settlers, eastern land speculators, soldiers with land warrants or certificates, as well as, as Ohio Company CEO Rufus Putnam at Marietta called them, "the poorer sort," seeking opportunities on

---

[26] "The Boundary Evolution of Roxbury Township, Washington County, Ohio," is given in Walker, *Stockport, Ohio: A Compendium of Historical Information*, (1984) pp. 37-9.
[27] Clyde Kean Swift, Muskingum Years, "1845."
[28] *The Spirit of Democracy*, Woodsfield, Ohio, January 17, 1846.

the western frontier, such as the defenseless settlers massacred by Indians at Big Bottom in 1791.

Robertson notes, "Probably the first store in [Windsor] township was kept by Richard Cheadle, on Big Bottom. He sold both dry and wet goods, having a distillery to supply the latter."[29] Although Asa's house stood on the Roxbury side of Lot #42 near the river (opposite the mouth of Mill Run),[30] the majority of his farm land was across the Muskingum, later widely known as the Buck Farm.

The names of all four Cheadle brothers, as do the names of virtually every male pioneer in that region—i.e., downriver from Windsor (i.e., Stockport), Big Bottom, Roxbury, Brokaw, Luke Chute, Swifts, and Center Bend—appear in bachelor, teacher, farmer, herbalist, and Yale College graduate (Class of 1777) Jonathan Baldwin's (1757–1816) *Day Books* in the early 1800s.[31] Richard Cheadle, for example, occasionally bought his wife's medicines from Baldwin. Those who could not pay cash (British or U.S.) bartered their goods, loaned him their plow horses, worked in his orchard, chopped wood, sawed and hauled his logs, and, in many instances, helped him pole his produce up the Muskingum to market at Zanesville. Baldwin's house stood on Lot #25, near the river (on its east side as it flows due north), in Waterford Township, Washington County, 1.4 miles north of present-day Luke Chute dam.

Brothers Asa and Richard Cheadle, according to Cheadle genealogists, were buried at Big Bottom Cemetery. Unfortunately, the 1913 flood wrecked the cemetery and most gravestones were irreparably damaged or lost. The river also swept away the tri-purpose Big Bottom schoolhouse, community center, and Protestant church. Ironically, the church's records survived the stone carved graves.

---

[29] Charles Robertson, *History of Morgan County*, Ohio, 1886, p. 407.
[30] See William D. Emerson, *Washington County, Ohio*, 1845. Map of Roxbury Township, p. 10. (Reprinted by the Washington County Historical Society, Marietta, Ohio, April 7, 1976.)
[31] Courtesy of Marietta College research librarian Linda Showalter.

Of the four Cheadle brothers who immigrated from Vermont to Ohio in 1799 and/or 1800, 19-year-old Paddock (Paddick was their mother Martha's maiden name in Vermont) was the youngest, strongest, and most eccentric. Although the year of their arrival at Marietta was 1799, 1800, or both, the brothers arrived in time to have their names recorded in the 1800 U.S. Census of the Northwest Territory in Waterford Township—except Paddock. Because he was not yet 21 years old, he is not listed by name, but by a pen stroke under "males not yet 21." Single at the time, Paddock

> …was a rather eccentric man and possessed of great muscular power. He eventually had a large orchard [on his Big Bottom farm] and took his apples and cider to Zanesville by keelboat. It is reported he could lift a barrel of cider from the ground and place it on a wagon.[32]

That is 42 gallons = 330+ lbs.! Although the muscular Paddock liked to wrestle, he never sought to hurt or cripple his opponents—he just squeezed them into submission. In one fracas with a bully in Zanesville, "When nothing else would do Paddock grabbed him and threw him to the ground and held him until he promised to behave under threat that he would squeeze the vinegar out of him."[33]

Young Paddock enlisted in the Ohio Militia during the War of 1812, presumably making him eligible for another U.S. land grant. Thus, the four Cheadle brothers from Vermont—Asa (b. 8/5/1762–9/13/1836), John, Sr. (b. 5/25/1771 in Connecticut–9/9/1823, buried at Round Bottom Cemetery near Coal Run), Richard (b. 7/23/1777–10/1830 buried at Roxbury [site unknown], and Paddock (b. 5/14/1780 in Vermont–5/26/1865 buried in Oregon)—by 1820 had been granted, bartered, or purchased four adjacent, 100-acre lots along the east side of the Muskingum, immediately west of the western boundary of the huge 100,000-acre Donation Tract, which was soon to be managed by

---

[32] Stanbery Alderman, "Slaves in Morgan County," *Morgan County Democrat*, Nov. 18, 1937, p. 5.
[33] George C. Williston, *A History of the Cheadle and White Families*, etc., circa 2005, pp. 69-70.

Rufus Putnam of the Ohio Company at Marietta, which the U.S. Congress set aside to be given to poor male settlers.[34]

That huge rectangular U.S. Donation Tract due east of the Cheadles' four adjacent 100-acre lots was not part of the Ohio Company Purchase in 1787. The U.S. Congress established it in 1792 in reaction to the Indians' destruction of the Big Bottom settlement (one mile downstream from present-day Stockport) and massacre of 12 settlers on January 2, 1791. Unlike the Ohio Company's land sales for profit, the Donation tract was surveyed at U.S. Government expense and the lots were given free to adult male migrants and war veterans under specific terms: He must own a gun, plant an orchard, build a house with a stone chimney and a stone cellar, live on the land five years, and, if ordered to do so, protect the Ohio Company settlers at Marietta, Belpre, and Waterford by repelling future Indian attacks.

Of the four white settlers the Indians took captive at Big Bottom, only one returned to the Ohio Company to live—James Patten (1754-1827). Held captive for four years in a Delaware village on the Auglaize River, he was presumed to have died. In fact, Delaware leader Big Cat (Whingwy Pooshies) owned and worked him as a slave. But after Patten's surprise discovery by U.S. soldiers during a nine-for-nine prisoner swap at Fort Defiance in January 1795, then his eventual return to Marietta, the Ohio Company, on March 8, 1797, granted Patten 100-acre Lot #40 at Big Bottom.[35] (See map, page 29.) Patten, however, did not live there. He sold Lot #40 on the Muskingum and moved near the mouth of Duck Creek to start a tree

---

[34] Today (2024) that westernmost border is the long, due-north portion of Michael Porter's farm lane. See enlargement of *1854 Map of Windsor Township Property Owners* on p. 50.

[35] James Patten's siblings in New Hampshire did not learn that he was alive and/or free for a long time—January 1791 until December 1795. In the interim, their father died. The Judge in New Hampshire held up distribution of his farm, land, and assets to heirs because he did not know if James was dead or alive. The New Hampshire judge, it turned out, was wise and just. Although Patten did not visit his relatives in New Hampshire until 1817, he received his share. (Phill Crane, "James Patten Honored today in Belpre," *Marietta Times*, September 26, 2015).

nursery.[36] Eventually he was a stonemason at Belpre, Ohio, where he died, January 31, 1827.[37]

On March 27, 1801, Asa Cheadle bought 300 acres (Lots #44, #45, and #46 in R11, T8) from Benjamin Dana for $900, located across the river from Roxbury (the future Buck Farm). Asa's younger brother John lived on and farmed it. "John Cheadle lived on what is now known as the Buck farm from the time of his settlement [in Ohio] until his death [in 1823]."[38] John and his wife Naomi (*nee* White), had four children: Rial, Electa,[39] Pamela,[40] and Gilman.[41] On December 1, 1801, John bought Benjamin Dana's narrow north-south 100-acre Lot #43, which spans part of the south bend of the river. The 25 acres on the south side included the future site of Roxbury and the 75 acres on the north side, where John built his house.[42]

Other than the four Cheadle brothers from Vermont, no attempt will be made to pursue local Cheadle genealogy. Why not? Consider, for example, Asa Cheadle, Sr., in the Roxbury area—he wed three times and sired 16 children! And to make it interesting, his twin daughters Tryphena and Tryphona married Olney brothers, Sylvanus and Oman, who lived a short distance down the Muskingum near Olive Green Creek. In 1807 Asa—a veteran of both the French and Indian War and the Revolutionary War—was elected, by a plurality of 24 of the 93 votes cast, to serve as one of two Justices of the Peace in Roxbury Township (then in Washington County, Ohio). Joseph Palmer, with 22 votes, was elected the other JP.[43]

---

[36] Former Big Bottom settler and long-term Indian captive James Patten is mentioned in horticulturist [Jonathan] *Baldwin's Day Books, 1794-1814*. See Book II, pp. 93-4 in 1806, and Book III in 1808, p. 14.
[37] Ironically, Belpre stonemason Patten's own grave and gravestone have not been found. He likely is buried in Cedarville Cemetery at Belpre which lies next to the Ohio River. Many of its grave markers have been lost or destroyed by floods over the centuries. A memorial marker was dedicated to Patten at the cemetery by the Belpre Historical Society on September 26, 2015.
[38] Robertson, *History of Morgan County, Ohio*, 1886, p. 393.
[39] "Lecty" Cheadle wed James Davis, Dec. 28, 1815. Both of Roxbury Co., Richard Cheadle, J.P.
[40] Pamela Cheadle wed Josiah Richmond, July 29, 1824. Both of Roxbury Co., Thomas White, J.P.
[41] Gilman Cheadle of Morgan Co. wed Susanna Rockey of Roxbury Co., March 13, 1828, Benjamin M. Brown of Wesley Township, J.P.
[42] Clyde K. Swift, *The Cheadle Family*, n.d.
[43] Williston, *op. cit.*, 2005, p. 58.

While serving as Justice of the Peace, in addition to marrying local couples, Asa officiated at his own relatives' weddings on at least five occasions between 1802 and 1817—a Cheadle wed by a Cheadle JP relative. Asa was buried in Big Bottom Cemetery, a few remnants of which are near the Muskingum in the southeast corner of Lot #100, now (2024) on the Steve Kosky property.

But, as fate would have it, due to the Muskingum River flood of 1913, Asa Cheadle, Sr., leader of the four-brother vanguard to Ohio, has no gravesite or marker.

* * * * * * * * *

Cheadle Family Ohio Property Tax Records in 1820

[A=acres R=Range T=Township S=Section L=Lot]

Asa	100A; R11 T9; L42, L46, L47.
John	100A; R11 T8; S17&18; L43.
	100A; R11 T8; S17&18; L42.
Paddock	100A; R11 T8; S17&18; L45.
	100A; R11 T9; S17&18; L91.
Richard	100A; R11 T8; S24; L100.
Joseph	100A; R11 T8; S—; L97.

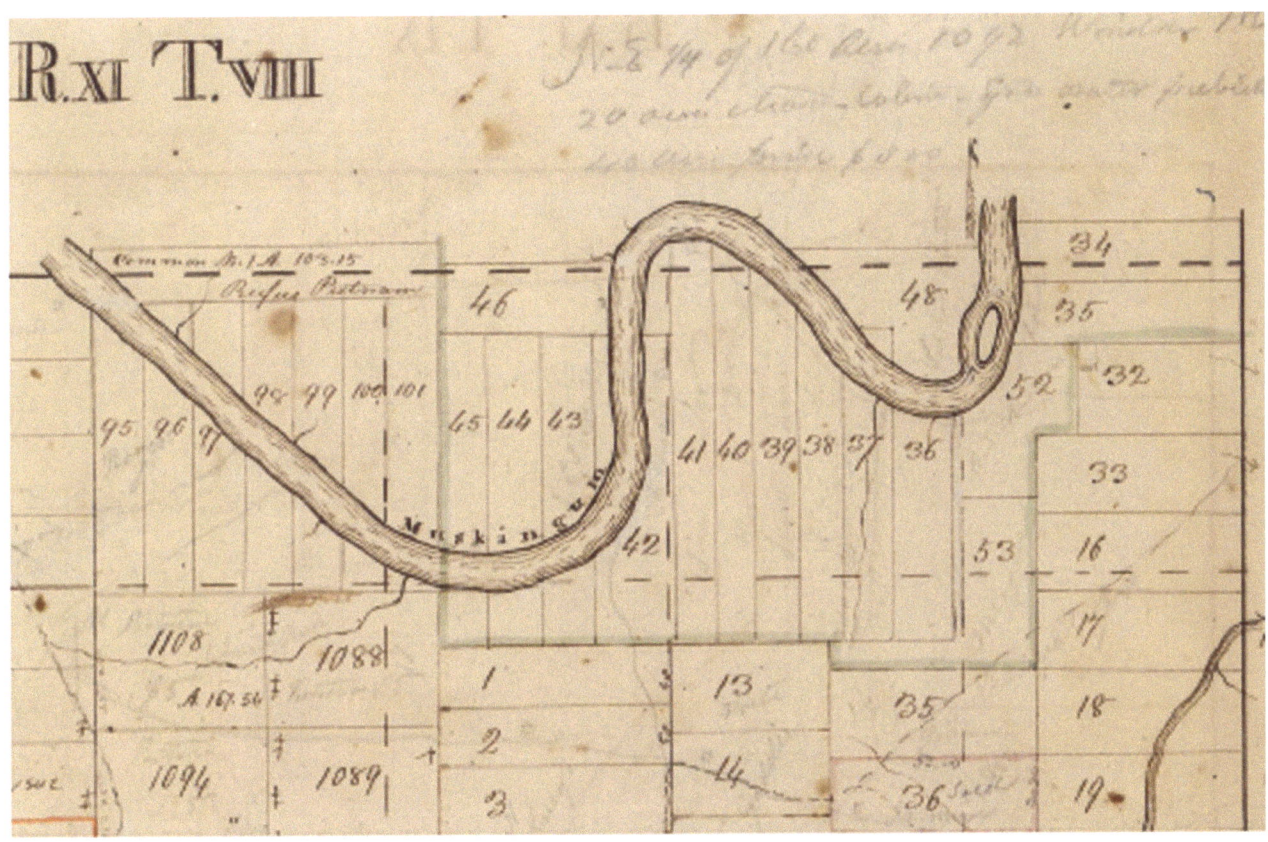

Enlarged view of R. XI, T. VIII, Lots #95-101, and Lots #41-52 (Ohio Company Map Collection, Marietta College)

N.B. Asa Cheadle, Sr. acquired 100A L#46 and 100A L#42 (shown in the center of the map above). However, the Muskingum River flows north down the middle of L#42, half of which is the river and its flood-prone and brush-covered banks. Asa's house (not shown) was located on that north-south sliver of **L#46** (top of map) lying on the east side of the Muskingum where it flows due north. When Asa died in 1836 he owned 400A, much of which later came to be known locally as The Buck Farm. Asa's brother John farmed it. John's son, Rial Cheadle, was born there in 1801.

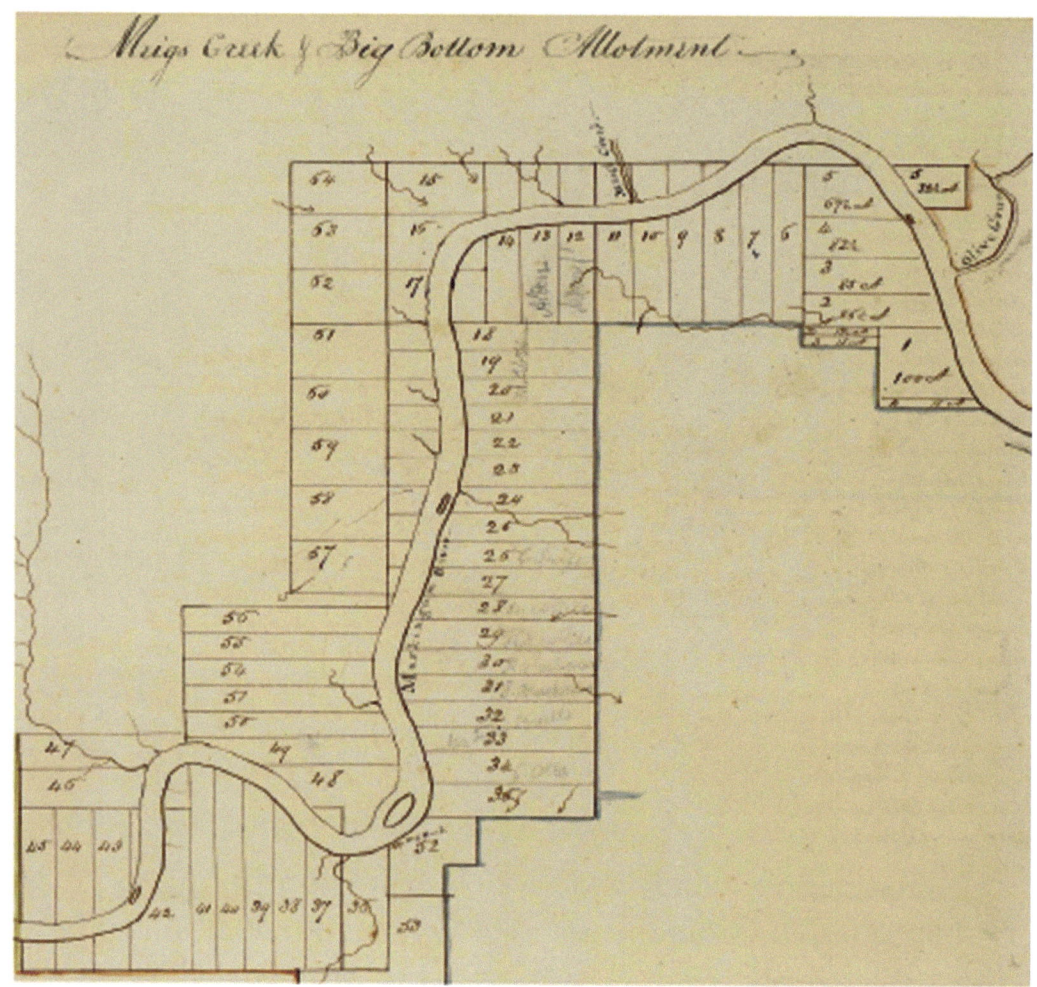

Meigs Creek & Big Bottom Allotment. (Lots #45-to-#36 are lower left). The former site of the "Big Rock," a noted Indian landmark which stood on the south bank of the river, is marked in Lot #52 (in fine print, bottom center). It was blasted apart when the railroad cut through Brokaw (a.k.a. Shacksville). Fragments of the rock are visible near the southeast shore only when the river is very low. As partial payment for his survey work, the Ohio Company granted Jeffery Mathewson Lot #37. N.B., Madison Run is shown in Lot #36, which is **an error.** (The map on page 29 shows it correctly—i.e., in Lot #37). Meigs Creek is center top (Lots #11 and #10); Olive Green Creek, named for early surveyors Robert Oliver and Griffin Greene, is at extreme upper-right (opposite 85-acre Lot #3). Mill Run is shown at extreme left, flowing due south, then southeast to the Muskingum very near the east-west boundary line between Lots #46 and #47 (lower left).

Notes on Big Bottom Landmarks

(See enlarged map of R9, T8 on page 29.)

L#96: Heading SE on SR266 from Stockport, only the very NE tip of L96 is north of the river.

L#97: A marble monument (set in 1905 bearing the names of the 12 Ohio Company settlers slain by Indians on January 2, 1791) stands in Big Bottom State Park near its north-south eastern boundary line.

L#98: Big Bottom School (church, and community center) stood in L98, near the N-S L#99 line on its east and down near the river.

L#99 and L#100: The Steve Kosky property with numerous alleys and cottages near the river.

L#100: Big Bottom Cemetery, near the river, is close to the L#101 line. Only a few markers remain.

L#101: Michael Porter farm: Bottoms near SR266 have been excavated for sand and gravel. The farm's easternmost north-south lot line (i.e., the north-south portion of Porter's long lane line between Lots #101 and #45) ends the original Ohio Company T-R land survey line numbering system of the early 1790s. The lots east of that line use the 1795 Donation Tract survey numbering system: West to east, they are 100A L#45, #44, #43, #42-36, etc..

* * *   * * *   * * *

"Now," as movie directors of old Hollywood westerns used to say, "Let's cut to the chase." Asa's son Cyrus (12/26/1786 in Barnard, Vermont—3/27/1850 buried in Big Bottom Cemetery), age 14, also came to Ohio with the four-brother vanguard in 1799/1800. On Valentine's Day in 1808—with his father, Asa, J.P., officiating—Cyrus wed Abigail (*nee* Van Clief) of Waterford Township. They had seven children. Their first—a son born at Roxbury—became, in adulthood, well-regarded Christopher Columbus ("Lum") Cheadle (4/13/1830–3/1914 buried at Waterford, Ohio). At age 67, Lum published the following remarkable family account in the *Marietta Daily Leader,* January 11, 1897. Entire and verbatim:

THAT SLAVE!

It Was Kate, the Dusky Maiden of Big Bottom

The statement having been made that there were at one time three negro slaves owned in Ohio, one each in Morgan, Noble and Washington counties, created some discussion and brings out a history of the Morgan county case from Mr. C. C. Cheadle, of Roxbury, up the Muskingum. He says: Paddock Cheadle, born in Barnard, Windham county, Vermont, May 14, 1780, moved to Ohio in the year 1800 and settled on Big Bottom, in Windsor township, on the farm now occupied by Henry Blackner [Blackmer]. Paddock Cheadle married Rachel Ankrum, of [Tyler County] Virginia [now West Virginia], in 1826, whose parents were wealthy slaveholders, and among the many gifts presented to the bride to set her up housekeeping in her new Ohio home, was Kate, a slave, then a young girl in her teens, from her looks a full blooded negro of the darkest type. Kate proved to be a valuable part of the outfit of housekeeping. Whether she ever knew that she was free when she crossed the Ohio river we can not say. However, she seemed reconciled to her new home and lived with the family all her days, content and happy. They sold their farm on Big Bottom and moved to [Marion Township,] Linn county, Ia., taking Kate with them. Whether this is the slave referred to or not it seems to fit the case. Perhaps others can give parallel cases of slaves being held in Morgan county.

Paddock Cheadle is listed in local Ohio property tax records in 1820, 1821, 1822, 1829, 1832, 1833, and 1837, and in each U.S. Census of Ohio up to and including 1840. Sometime after the 1840 U.S. Census, Ohio homesteader Paddock, his wife Rachel Ankrum (or Ankrom), and their three children pulled up stakes, left Big Bottom, and moved to Linn County, Iowa. In the 1840 Census of Ohio Paddock listed one boy under age 5; one boy 5-10; one male 20-30; one girl 5-10; one woman 20-30; one woman 40-50; and, under "Free Colored Persons," one female 10-24. She, no doubt, was Kate. But that was not true—*she was not free.*

Who was she? Kate was born and raised among the slaves of Tyler County, Virginia (now West Virginia) slave owner Jacob Duckett Ankrom, whose plantation was up the Ohio River from Marietta across from the easternmost end of Washington County, Ohio. When, how, where, and why Paddock first met Rachel Ankrum is not known. (Their Virginia marriage license spells her name "Ankrom.") As noted, when Paddock, age 45, and Rachel, age 35, wed on June 8, 1826, Rachel's father, Jacob D. Ankrom, among his wedding gifts, gave one of his slaves, a young girl named Kate, to his daughter Rachel as a wedding present, but with a special stipulation. Three years earlier, Ankrom, failing in health, had written in his "Last Will and Testament," dated October 1, 1823:

> I give and bequeath to my daughter Rachel my Negro girl Cate, my young horse two beds and be[d]ding one bureau two cows five sheep and two hogs on the day of her marriage or the marriage or death of my wife Nancy which ever first happens. Nevertheless it is not my desire that the said Negro Cate should serve as a slave longer than during the said Rachel's natural life.[44]

Virginia slave owner Jacob Ducket Ankrom died nine days later. Thus, when Paddock Cheadle's wife Rachel died, Kate by law would be free. When and where did Rachel die? Rachel (1/28/1790–11/17/1861), died, age 71, in Linn County, Iowa, and is buried there in Oak Shade Cemetery. On that day, Kate, if she were yet living, became legally free–or should have been. Where was Kate when her white mistress Rachel, for the prior 35 years, died in 1861?

Efforts to find Kate's grave—or even a notice, date, place of death, or any other document referring to her in or after 1840 in Iowa—have thus far failed. Presumably, given that Columbus Cheadle mentioned her having lived with the family "all her days," Kate died at or near Cedar Rapids, Iowa. Repeating: When Kate's governess, Paddock Cheadle's wife, died in Linn County, Iowa, on November 17, 1861, Kate was "free at last," if she were yet alive. When did Kate die? Of what?

---

[44] *West Virginia Will Books*, 1756-1971.

Was she ever freed? Where is she buried? Only one of the three Cheadle family genealogies at hand addresses those questions. Cheadle descendant George C. Williston of Hastings, Michigan, in *A History of the Cheadle and White Families of Early Washington and Morgan Counties, Ohio, Pre-Statehood Vermont and Ohio Families*, first published in the Washington County, Ohio, Historical Society journal *Tallowlight*, then later in his Cheadle family genealogy booklet in October 2005, addresses those questions. Williston states:

> Through the influence of a Methodist minister he [Paddock Cheadle] married a lady in Virginia by the name of Rachel Aukman [sic], a slave holder's daughter. Rachel's parents gave her a good setting out for housekeeping among other things and perhaps the most prized was a colored servant named Kate who proved to be a good helpmate for the family. She was perhaps the only slave ever held in the state of Ohio. She probably knew she was free but being greatly attached to her mistress was contented and apparently happy. They afterwards moved to Iowa. Kate lived to a great age and died and was buried beside her mistress whom she loved. A beautiful slab was placed at her grave to mark the resting place of this faithful servant.[45]

"Lived to a great age"! How great? When did she die? "Slab marker!" Where? Although Find-A-Grave shows Rachel Cheadle's grave in Iowa, a "beautiful slab" marking Kate's grave "beside her mistress," or *any* other information about Kate in Iowa has yet to be found.

---

[45] Williston, *op. cit.*, 2005, p. 70. Rachel (*nee* Aukrom/Akrum) Cheadle is buried in Oak Shade Cemetery in Marion, Iowa, in the Pioneer Section, Lot 25, Space #3, age 71. Courtesy of the good folks in Marion via email in 2023-24. Kate's gravesite has not yet been located.

Question Number 10:

What Became of Restless Paddock Cheadle and His Family?

After nearly two decades growing to young manhood in Vermont, three decades homesteading in Ohio, and two decades homesteading in Iowa, in 1862 restless Paddock, at age 70, and his three children born at Big Bottom [Lamar, 1827–1901; Raphael, 1829–1918; and Miranda Elnora (*nee* Cheadle) Craig (1833–1915)] sold out, pulled up stakes again, loaded their wagons, and trudged up the Oregon Trail to homestead a *third* time—near Shedd, Oregon. The arduous trip, one family record states, "took nearly six months." Richard Cheadle went with them.

They then moved to Harney County where several of Paddock's descendants are now buried. Paddock (5/14/1780–5/26/1865) died, age 85, and is buried in Riverside Cemetery overlooking Calapooya Creek, in Albany, Linn County, Oregon. A Methodist Episcopal Church record at nearby Shedd, the community where they had originally settled, notes, "Paddock Cheadle Died in the faith 1864 [sic)]." No. As his tombstone makes clear: He died May 26, 1865.

Regarding the fate of Kate, the Cheadles left one clue back in Iowa. It reminds one of Sherlock Holmes' clue, "The dog that didn't bark." The Census of Marion Township, Linn County, Territory of Iowa, 1854, lists the "Paddic [sic] Cheadle" family as having only two members: "1 white male, 1 white female, 0 children, 0 colored males, and 0 colored females." Presumably, Kate had not lived to a great age, but died before the 1854 Iowa Census. But thanks to "Lum" Cheadle of Roxbury, Ohio, in 1897 and Cheadle genealogist George Williston of Hastings, Michigan, in 2005, Kate is gone, but not forgotten.

Questions Number 11 and Number 12:

Who Built the First House on the Future Site of Stockport, Lot #90?
Who Was the First White Child Born on the Future Site of Stockport?

Dr. Charles Robertson's *History of Morgan County, Ohio*, published in 1886,[46] offers two possibilities for the first white child born at the pre-1834 Stockport site: 1) An **Eveland** child or 2) a **Lucas** child born between 1811 and 1834, the latter the year the town was platted and lots offered for sale.

Examination of **Theory One**: An **Eveland** child.

> Frederick Eveland [Jr.] was born in 1764 in Newbury, New Jersey, and died December 20, 1854, in Bloomington, Illinois. He wed in Tioga County, New York, in 1786 and subsequently brought his wife and their children from New York via Pennsylvania to Ohio and settled where Stockport now is in 1811. He occupied a double log cabin, in one room of which he kept saloon, while his wife, a religious woman, lived and frequently had religious meetings in another room. Neither meddled with the affairs of the other, and they lived harmoniously together. Frederick's sons, Nathaniel, David, Moses, and John and several daughters, were also residents of the township. Nathaniel Lucas, a blacksmith by trade, settled in the same neighborhood in 1811.[47]

Notice that Robertson did not mention Frederick Eveland's wife's name! He describes her character and religious beliefs, but states neither her name nor origin. How unusual! Why not? Racial prejudice? Her name was Lois Evans (1768-1849).[48] She came to Ohio from Tioga County, New York (midway between Elmira and Binghamton), and was one-quarter American Indian. Was her Indian heritage the reason Robertson omitted her name? Lois Evans' genealogy (Ancestry.com):

---
[46] Robertson, *op. cit.*, 1886, p. 401.
[47] Robertson, *op. cit.*, 1886, p. 401; insert of data from other sources are in brackets.
[48] Material submitted by Barbara L. Covey, 1996. See Appendix G.

Lois Evans was born in Damascus, Wayne County, Pennsylvania. Her one-quarter Indian heritage stemmed from her full-blooded Indian grandmother on her father's side. Her father, Nathaniel Evans (1742-1820), was born across the Delaware River from Pennsylvania in Cochecton, New York. He, half-Indian, half-white, came to Ohio, too, but little is known about his later years in Ohio, except that he worked as a laborer in Marietta, died in 1820, and is buried in Mound Cemetery in Marietta! Why Mound Cemetery?[49] *He, half-Delaware, half-white, was a Revolutionary War veteran who fought for the Americans!* (His white wife's name was Sarah Thomas.) In turn, Nathaniel's mother (i.e., Lois' grandmother) was Maria Evans, a full-blooded Indian. "Marie" Evans is among the twelve Delaware women living at Bethlehem, Pennsylvania, recorded by missionary Reverend David Zeisberger on November 15, 1756. As well, Zeisberger listed Lois' son "Nett" (short for Nathaniel) among the ten Indian boys also living there.[50]

But were *both* of Maria's parents full-blooded Indians? Yes. Maria was the daughter of Johnathan Cayenguerego (or Cayenquiliquo) (1696-1763) and his wife Maria Kejenjketchachtado (born 12/26/1723 in Anderson, Orange County, New York—died 1757). They both were full-blooded Delaware Indians. May this help give Lois Evans the recognition long overdue her and her multiracial descendants, past and present, in Stockport, in Morgan County, in the Muskingum Valley, in Ohio, and beyond—and give a fresh meaning to those generations in school at Stockport who were proud to be called "Windsor Indians."

Frederick Eveland, Jr., liked terraced Lot #90 on the west side of the Muskingum, but so did a lot of men. On October 16, 1816, he bought the entire 100-acre lot

---

[49] "[At] Mound Cemetery on Fifth Street [in Marietta, Ohio] the map marker on the right at the base of the [Indian] Mound locates the known graves of the Revolutionary soldiers in this cemetery while nearby to the left of the main walk is the D.A.R. memorial plot. This has individual bronze markers with flag holders for those soldiers who died in . . . Washington County but whose actual graves have not been found. . . . It [has been] verified that Nathan Evans was indeed buried in Mound Cemetery but since the exact site is not known he is honored in the D.A.R. memorial plate with a flag holder and a name plate bearing the date 1742-1820. —Nathaniel Evans: A Frontier Soldier,'" (Elizabeth S. Cottle, *Tallow Light*, Vol. 20, No. 2, p. 67, n.d. Courtesy of Linda Showalter, Marietta College, Marietta, Ohio. 2023)
[50] *Pennsylvania Archives*, Vol. III, 1853, pp. 52-3.

from Nicholas Longworth for $500.[51] Indicative of the rampant speculation in rich Muskingum River bottom land in the pioneer era, Eveland was the sixth owner of Lot #90 in only 11 years.[52] But the key question remains: Were any of Eveland's eight children born there between 1811 and 1834?

Answer: No. The first five of Frederick, Jr., and Lois (*nee* Evans) Eveland's eight children were born in Toiga County, New York; only the last three—Amy, John, and Elizabeth—were born in Ohio. Where and when? Amy was born in Washington County in 1796; John was born in Waterford Township in 1800; and Elizabeth was born in 1802 in Washington County—thus, all three were born before 1811, the year Robertson states their parents moved to the pre-Stockport site. Thus, the first-child-born-at-pre-Stockport Eveland hypothesis is not supported.

As well, their son Nathaniel Eveland, according to Robertson,[53] lived "Opposite the site . . . of Stockport," likely the late John or Chet Porter farms. It is noted in passing that three Eveland children wed local Newtons—David wed Nancy, John wed Harriet, and Catherine wed Walter Newton.[54]

Theory Two: A **Lucas** child. Note that Robertson in 1886 added at the end of his Eveland family paragraph quoted earlier: "Nathaniel Lucas, a blacksmith by trade, settled in the same neighborhood [as the Evelands, also] in 1811."[55] Examination of the Lucas theory:

> Nathaniel Lucas, was born at Hartford, Connecticut, July 19, 1772; and died August 16, 1855. In his native place he learned the trade of blacksmith, and engaged in that business in building ships until he was twenty-two years of age

---

[51] Walker, *Stockport, Ohio*, 1984, pp. 64-5.
[52] A chronology of the landowners of the pre-Stockport half of Lot #90 is given in Appendix A.
[53] Robertson, *History of Morgan County, Ohio*, p. 392.
[54] Walker, *Stockport, Ohio*, 1984, p. 234. As one Stockport wit warned me decades ago when I was researching local material for the book, *Wolf Creek and the Muskingum*, "Be careful who you criticize around here—you're probably related!" Today I would quip: "Yes. And maybe even part Indian—and proud of it! Weren't we the Windsor Indians?"
[55] Robertson, *op. cit.*, p. 401.

[1794], when he emigrated to Marietta, Ohio, where he carried on the business of blacksmithing, and assisted in ironing the first ships built at that place. In 1797 he married Elizabeth Robinson [1779-1870], daughter of Lieut. William Robinson, of Washington county, then territory of Ohio . . . .

Nathaniel Lucas continued to reside at Marietta after his marriage, doing the blacksmith work in the ship yard for four years. In those days the country was infested with savage Indians, and it was not safe to travel alone. He removed to Roxbury [Township], on Wolf Creek, at the mouth of one of its tributaries, which to this day is called Lucas Run, where he continued blacksmithing until the year 1845, when his eyesight began to fail him. [*Hence, a decade or more after Stockport was platted in 1834*]. He gave it up and turned his attention to farming. In after years he located in Morgan county, where the town of Windsor [Stockport] now stands. Nathaniel and Elizabeth [*nee* Robinson] Lucas were the parents of 11 children: Nancy, William B., Jane, Jalana, Charles R., Albert C., Clarinda, Josiah S., Mary, Fannie, and Harriet. The first two were born at Ft. Harmar, opposite Marietta. Elizabeth (*nee* Robinson) survived her husband until October 8, 1870. They both passed the last years of their lives with their son, Albert C. Lucas in Gallia county, and were buried at Vinton [Ohio][56] …

By 1820 Nathaniel Lucas, age 48, was living in Windsor Township; likewise, in 1830. Of the five Lucas children born in Ohio, only one was born between 1811 and 1834—Albert C. Lucas, born in 1816. But an ancestral record explicitly states that he was born at Marietta. Albert Lucas died in 1884. Thus, the **Lucas child theory is also eliminated.**[57]

---

[56] Text slightly rearranged for clarity. *History of the Upper Ohio Valley*, Vol. II, 1891, pp. 352-3.
[57] On March 5, 1797, the Ohio Company at Marietta granted the four Lucas brothers [William, Samuel, Nathaniel, Joseph] four adjacent Ohio Company lots along the West Branch of Wolf Creek. [*Wolf Creek and the Muskingum*, 1996, p. 366] Perchance Nathaniel Lucas' brother, William of Waterford Township, was the first white owner of the lot on which the present-day Waterford Boy Scout Troop's log house on the West Branch of Wolf Creek yet stands [2024] in Windsor Township, Morgan County, Ohio. The log house was built on Lot #17 by its owner William Hook circa 1843-45. One early owner is reputed to have kept a pet bear at the site.

That leaves **Theory Three**: A Cheadle son or daughter. And that requires examination of the Cheadle family's claim as to the first white child born at the site of pre-Stockport.

Paddock and his brother Richard were not the only Cheadle brothers to speculate in land at the future site of Stockport. So did their older brother John, who lived down the Muskingum at the Buck Farm near present-day Luke Chute Dam. Cheadle descendants claim that the first house built on the site of pre-Stockport was a hewn log cabin built in 1818 or 1820 by John's son, Rial Cheadle, who, as noted, when a young man, was an early teacher at the first school in Morgan County, located at Big Bottom. Rial was 15 years old when his mother, Naomi (*nee* White) Cheadle, died in February, 1816.

Big Bottom School stood on Lot #98, about 1.8 miles down SR266 from Stockport. The site of the schoolhouse is precisely known via an early panoramic photograph of the Muskingum Valley. As well, its location is marked "SH" on local maps in 1869, 1875, and 1880, and as "Sch No. 1" on a map in 1902.[58] As noted, the Muskingum River flood in 1913 destroyed the schoolhouse, virtually all of Big Bottom Cemetery, and destroyed or ruined most of the houses and structures in Roxbury. Also noted, Rial (b. 9/30/1801 at the Buck farm; d. 9/21/1867 buried at McConnelsville) was a son of John Cheadle and his wife Naomi (*nee* White, 9/13/1771–2/1816).

On March 5, 1820, Rial Cheadle and Mary Tufts[59] wed in, "Olive [?] Township, Morgan County, Ohio," by Minister William Davis (who spelled Rial "Royal" and Tufts "Tuft").[60] Rial and Mary (b. 11/17/1800 at Belfast, Maine–d. 10/21/1827) had one

---

[58] Connie (*nee* Jones) and Norman Pillsbury, *Big Bottom Explorations*, 2009, pp. 23ff.
[59] Mary Tufts was the daughter of Thomas and Dorothy (*nee* Davidson) Tufts. Tom was born May 27, 1774, in Belfast, Maine. Dorothy was born March 3, 1777, at Lowell, Massachusetts.
[60] Olive Township is unknown to the author. Perhaps they did not wed in Morgan County, Ohio.

son and two daughters: Thomas Dinsmore (1821-1903), Armenta (1822-????), and Francina (1824-1883).[61]

Armenta wed Edward Woods (1818) in Muskingum County, Ohio, on August 7, 1840. He apparently died shortly thereafter. Armenta then married Andrew Kessinger on April 6, 1848. Her burial place and date of death have not been found. [Family Search]

YOUR NOTES

---

[61] FamilySearch.org

Rial Cheadle   1801–1867

Question Number 13:

Why Have the Names of Rial and Mary (*nee* Tufts) Cheadle's Two Daughters Been Kept a Family Secret?

Cheadle family genealogists George Williston (2005), Jean Minish-Stoner (1977), and Clyde K. Swift (circa 1989), as well as major histories and biographies, such as H. Z. Williams' *History of Washington County, Ohio,* in 1881, and Morgan County (such as Judge James Gaylord's *Reminiscences* in 1873 and Charles Robertson's *History of Morgan County, Ohio* in 1886) cite Rial and Mary's son, Thomas Dinsmore Cheadle, but do not mention Thomas Cheadle's two younger sisters, also likely born at pre-Stockport circa 1822 and 1824. Why their names have been omitted for more than 150 years is unknown. As well, it is clear their omissions were neither a family oversight nor due to erroneous Internet postings. [See: Family Search]

One fact—Tom's unique middle name, "Dinsmore"—illustrates the puzzle. Neither Rial Cheadle nor his wife Mary Tufts had any known in-laws or ancestors named or surnamed Dinsmore. Thus, this theory arises by default: "Dinsmore" was indeed a common family surname in the area of Vermont where the four Cheadle brothers, their parents, and their ancestors had lived long before the four brothers emigrated to Ohio in 1799/1800. Perhaps the Dinsmore and Cheadle families in New England, though not blood relatives, were especially close friends. For example, the Dinsmores of Vermont and the early Fryes at Beverly, Ohio, were directly related.

The name "Dinsmore" had a special meaning in the Cheadle family. Consider: Rial and Mary never mentioned that their daughter Francina Cheadle wed Amos M. Rose (1821-1904) in 1842. The Rose family lived in Iowa and Francina is buried in Ionia Cemetery in Iona, Kansas. In turn, Francina (*nee* Cheadle) and Amos Rose named their son Rial Dinsmore Rose (1851-1930)! In turn, Rial Dinsmore Rose wed

Jane A. Catlin (1852-1943) and they named their son Rial Catlin Rose (1882-1924), who received his Ph.D. in botany at the University of Chicago in 1917.

The multi-generational transmission of the unique name "Rial" indicates that Francina was indeed a daughter of Rial Cheadle. So why has she been omitted from family records? Yet, why was the name "Dinsmore" repeated for generations by those who never lived in New England? Why the silence regarding her pre-Stockport sister Armenta, who married Edward Woods (1818-xxxx) in 1840 in Muskingum County and named their son Thomas Densmore [with an "e"] Woods (1842-1912)? Why the silence among Cheadle family genealogists? After Woods died, Armenta wed Andrews Kessinger on April 6, 1848, at Fairfield, Ohio. After that, Armenta's trail turns cold near Gibisonville (pop. 130), near Logan, Ohio. [See Ancestry.com]

Also odd: Rial Cheadle and his second wife, Elizabeth Sands (a.k.a. Sanns), while living near Ringgold in Union Township, Morgan County, Ohio, had one child: Mary Jane Cheadle (1842-1862). Apparently, Jane did not marry or have children. Why did she die at age 20? Where? Where is her grave? Why is she neither cited nor mentioned in any of the four Cheadle family genealogies at hand?

In 1924 Thomas Dinsmore Cheadle's son (Rial's grandson), a tailor by trade, William Dean Cheadle of Utica, Ohio, asserted in the *Morgan County Democrat*:

> Rial Cheadle. . . was married in 1819 and soon after built his home—a log cabin—where my father, Thomas D. [Dinsmore] Cheadle was born. This was the first house built in what is now known as Stockport, and my father, Thomas D. Cheadle, bears the distinction of being the first white child born in Stockport.[62]

In 1833 Rial Cheadle taught at Big Bottom School, the first public school in what is now Morgan County. Because he and fellow teacher Bennet Roberts staunchly

---
[62] *Morgan County Democrat*, July 24, 1924, p. 8.

opposed slavery, the school was known locally as "The Abolition School." After Rial's first wife, Mary Tufts, died in 1827, Rial became a secret conductor on the Underground Railroad in the decades leading up to the Civil War.[63]

Two years after the Civil War ended, Rial's secret work done and slavery abolished, "He," wrote Rial's grandson, William Dean Cheadle of Utica, Ohio, in 1924, "died at the home of his son, Thomas Dinsmore Cheadle, in McConnelsville in 1867, and lies buried in the McConnelsville cemetery."[64]

Rial was indeed an energetic, clever, courageous, talented, and dedicated freedom fighter for the civil rights of all Americans. Consider, for example, Rial's insouciant reply to the U.S. Census-taker in Union Township, Morgan County, Ohio, in 1860, on the eve of the Civil War:

> Name: Ryal [sic] Cheadle
> Age: 64
> Sex: Male
> Occupation: Asst. Fugitive Slaves

What an amazing person! Who among us—having knowingly, intentionally, secretly, and repeatedly violated U.S. federal law for the past 20+ years—would tell a U.S. census official it was his or her occupation! Although his various secret, dangerous, and extensive activities are too voluminous to recount here, one of Rial's well-known and widely celebrated accomplices, Thomas L. Gray of Deavertown, Ohio—*the* major underground "station" for fugitive slaves in southeastern Ohio fleeing to freedom in Canada—later said of Rial:

> Mrs. Lydia Stokely fed fugitives [at her home], it was one of Rial Cheadle's stopping places. This Rial Cheadle is head and shoulders above me as a conductor,

---

[63] See Robertson, *History of Morgan County, Ohio*, 1886, pp. 150-56.
[64] *Morgan County Democrat*, July 24, 1924, p. 8.

engineer and baggage master. He has taken more risks and done more traveling twice over than I ever did. Often he has called on me with fugitives at most all hours of the night, got a bit to eat and then going on, stopping in the vicinity of Zanesville. After the freedom of the slaves, he called on me and stayed some three or four days, saying he felt like old Simeon — if the lord was willing he would like to depart. I never saw him again. He died shortly after he was at my house.[65]

Decades later, in 1892, Martha Millions, a Quaker woman at Pennsville, Ohio, wrote to W. H. Seibert, an Ohio State University professor who, in the late 1880s and 1890s, was documenting the history of the Underground Railroad in Ohio:

> ...Cheadle, first having built a cabin in 1818 or 1820 on the present site of the village of Stockport, Ohio. He afterwards became a teacher, then . . . became entirely devoted to the work of the Underground Railroad.

Entirely and heroically devoted, indeed! Consider this final remarkable tribute:

> In 1893 Mr. H. C. Harvey, then of Manchester, Kansas, but formerly of Morgan County, Ohio, who was involved in the Underground Railroad between 1850-1861, tells the following after telling of a family Rial had brought up through to Deavertown:

> Mr. Cheadle was a second John Brown in courage and determination and he declared that a government founded on an equal and exact justice to all should not longer live a life by permitting American Slavery. He was the most indefatigable conductor in Ohio and no history of the URR of Ohio would be complete without a biographical sketch of him.[66]

Should not every school student in Morgan County, Ohio—especially in Windsor, Penn, Marion, York, Deerfield, Union, Homer, and Malta townships—be required

---

[65] George C. Williston, *A History of the Cheadle and White Families*, 2005, pp. 85-6.
[66] Quote is in Williston, *op. cit.*, p. 86.

to learn about Rial Cheadle, his heroic deeds, and visit this intelligent, noble, and courageous man's modest grave in McConnelsville? Given that Rial was born September 30, 1801, in Morgan County should not the Morgan County Board of Education make a day in late September, "Rial Cheadle Day," in all public schools?

If not we, who? If not now, when? Yes, 2024 is late—but a lot sooner than never.[67]

YOUR NOTES

---

[67] See photograph of Rial Cheadle on p. 42.

Question Number 14:

Who Is the First Person Known to Have Died at or near pre-Stockport Lot #90?

Silverheels—a brother of Shawnee Chief Cornstalk, of their oft-noted sister Nonhelema, and of subchief Nimwha—was killed by a son of Abel Sherman—either Ezra ("Eli") or Josiah—probably in summer 1798. Where? Although accounts vary, Silverheels was likely murdered at or near his campsite which was near the mouth of Bald Eagle Creek [in Lot #89] near pre-Stockport. Why?

Sometime in the late 1790s, Silverheels boasted around the campfire at the then well-known salt boilers' camp (near present-day Chandlersville, Ohio) that, during the Indian war (1790-1795), he had been in a raiding party that had slain and scalped a white settler upriver from Beverly who had a double-crown of hair, making the scalp, when divided in two, twice as valuable when sold to the British "hair buyers" at Detroit. But, because militiamen from Fort Frye were fast approaching to counterattack the Indians, Silverheels could not flee rapidly and carry the slain farmer's rifle as well as his own. So, said he, he hid the farmer's gun in the rotted trunk of a nearby tree, intending to retrieve it later.

Unknown to Silverheels, one of Abel Sherman's sons was among the salt boilers listening intently to his tale. He (which brother has never been identified) later returned to the family farm and found his father's gun inside a rotted tree trunk. Proof positive—case closed. Although killing an Indian was by then clearly murder, not long after Silverheels' boast, his body was found near his well-known Bald Eagle campsite. Who killed him and when are still officially unknown.[68] One account summarizes:

---

[68] An old, rusted, pioneer-era rifle was on display at Campus Martius Museum for decades as that which may have belonged to Abel Sherman. More recently, the Museum has changed hands and its historical focus. What became of the rifle is apparently (2023) unknown. (Courtesy of Jean Yost, Cutler, Ohio.)

"There [near the mouth of Bald Eagle Creek] Silverheels had lived and there he died, and there was a father's death avenged; and now the deepened water of the river [due to the construction of dams] hides the memorial of his name [i.e., Silverheels Riffle adjacent Silverheels Farm and across the river from the mouth of Turkey Run below Stockport]."[69]

YOUR NOTES

---

[69] Robertson, *Op. cit.*, 1886, p. 97. Also, in Walker, *Where Is the Legendary Silverheels?*, 1980, p. 56; James M. Gaylord, *Historical Reminiscences of Morgan County [Ohio]*, pre-1884 (reprint 1984), pp. 23-4. Earlier still, Marietta doctor and historian Samuel P. Hildreth also repeats the Silverheels saga. The Schaad family, owner (2024) of Silverheels Farm, has dropped its historic Indian name. The farm house is now called *Mary's House* and serves as a temporary home for unwed mothers.

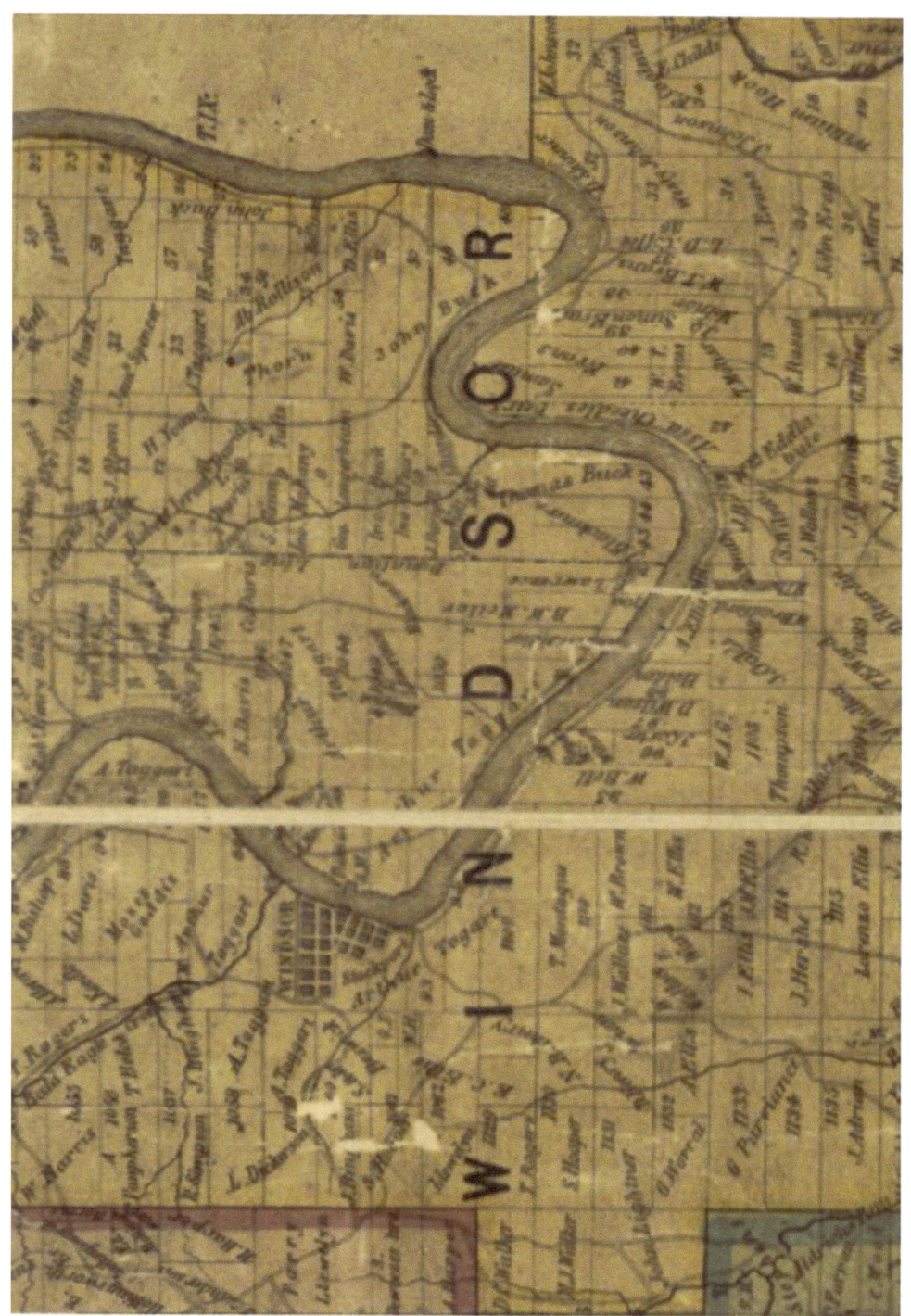

Landowners in central Windsor Township in 1854. N.B. Windsor and Stockport are labeled separately. Arthur Taggart was the largest land owner in Morgan County in that era. Note his large acreage on all four sides of Stockport. The north-south (western) "Donation Line" is near the big "S." The U.S. government gave the land east of that line free to settlers.

Question Number 15:

Who Was the First White Woman Who Died at the pre-Stockport Site?

Rial Cheadle's first wife, Mary Tufts, was born November 17, 1800, in Belfast, Maine.[70] She died in 1827—seven years before the village was platted in 1834—*presumably* in the family log house at pre-Stockport. *If* correct, she was quite likely the first white woman who died at pre-Stockport. Unfortunately, site of the Cheadle log house at Stockport is unknown.

Although the cause of her death is unknown, in 1931 Eck Humphries noted in the Preface of his excellent booklet on Rial Cheadle and his activities in *The Underground Railroad*:

> Mary Tufts Cheadle died in 1827 and now [1931] lies buried on the old Thomas Mummey, now the Susan Lyne [Lyons?] farm, in East Windsor.[71]

YOUR NOTES

---

[70] Ancestry.com
[71] Presumably, the Mummey Cemetery is the cemetery at the Fairview Methodist Protestant Church, located in the extreme northeast corner of 100-acre Lot #16 (owned by "T. Mummy" in 1854) in Windsor Township east of Stockport. The Church stands in the fork where, when driving north on Point Lookout Road (CR36), Kirkpatrick Lane, also heading north from the southwest, merges with CR36. The cemetery is behind (i.e., south of) the church, therefore is also in the fork between the junction of the two roads. The cemetery now consists of about 100 tombstones, many others obviously missing, damaged, or illegible. No list of burials has been found. [Research courtesy of Steve Hanson of East Windsor (Emails, 2023). A full view of the 1854 map of Windsor Township landowners, part of which is shown on page 50, is on the Internet. Search: William P. Johnson, *Map of Morgan County, Ohio*, 1854.

Question Number 16:

Who Was the First White Child Born at the pre-Stockport Site?

With both the Eveland family and the Lucas family hypotheses eliminated, the answer is no surprise. As quoted, Cheadle descendants and genealogists claim that the first white child born at the future site of Stockport was the son of Rial Cheadle by his first wife Mary Tufts. However, one early record, presented below, clearly contradicts the Cheadle family's claim.

Mary was a charter member of the First Baptist Church of Roxbury, which later merged with the Brick Church north of Stockport.[72] "Here," says a family record, "Thomas D. [Dinsmore] Cheadle was born [December 16, 1821] and was the first white child born in Stockport."[73] Tom was about six years old when his mother, Mary (*nee* Tufts), died in 1827, cause unknown. Tom's sisters, Francina and Arimenta [Armenta], were two and four years younger.

Another author states in 1931:

> At Stockport Rial followed the trade of a carpenter, a maker of pewter buttons and a hunter. A few years after the death of his first wife, he became a teacher, teaching subscription schools in Windsor, Marion, Union, and Homer townships [in Morgan County]. On July 11, 1840, with Isaiah Shepard, J.P., officiating, he married widow Rebecca "Betty" Sands, who lived west of Ringgold on the Emery Updike farm. Here for the next three decades, Rial pursued his Underground activities, his journeys being made in the intervals of school teaching and farming. It is believed that the Underground Railroad work of Rial Cheadle extended over 30 years and that while living in Windsor

---

[72] Charles Robertson, *History of Morgan County, Ohio*, 1886, p. 412. The First Baptist Church of Roxbury, across the river from the village of Roxbury, was the same building as the Big Bottom School and the Community Center in that early era. Revivals lasting weeks were held there.
[73] *Morgan County Democrat*, July 24, 1924, p. 8.

township and before the death of his first wife, he was interested in the Emancipation movement. He died at the home of his son, Thomas D. Cheadle, in McConnelsville in 1867 and is buried in the McConnelsville cemetery.[74] Their marriage certificate states, "Rial wed Elizabeth Sanns [Sands] in Morgan County, on July 11, 1839. Isaiah Shepard, J.P." Oddly, Justice of the Peace Shepard took pains to note on their marriage certificate that he, too, was 38 years old!

Who Built the First House in Stockport?

On June 11, 1942, The Morgan County Democrat [page 5 of 8], published the following information supplied by "the venerable Henry Hook," [born January 20, 1858, died April 2, 1944 in Chicago, buried at Stockport], son of famous Civil War steamboat Captain Isaac ("Ike") Newton Hook of Stockport and his wife Lucinda (nee Dearborn) who lived at Hooksburg:

> Mr. Hook showed us a poem written by Rial Cheadle in memory of Joel Sherman. Many years later W. D. Cheadle of Utica [Ohio] had it put in print. In fact we find the sheet bears the date February 15, 1924. Joel Sherman was married in 1819 and soon after built a log cabin in what is now the village of Stockport, which is said to have been the first house and home in the village. [See Question #28.]

YOUR NOTES

---

[74] Eck Humphries, *The Underground Railroad*, 1931, see his Preface.

Question Number 17:

What Became of pre-Stockport's First Known Native Son, Thomas Dinsmore Cheadle?

Thomas Dinsmore Cheadle married Dorcas (*nee* Neely) of Neelysville on March 28, 1845. He was a tailor by trade and lived in McConnelsville where he owned a tailor shop on Lot #45 in the Buckeye Block on Center Street. He was also apparently a member of the Masonic Lodge in Malta.

In June, 1863, age 42, he enlisted in the Union Army. Nine years after the end of the Civil War, for reasons unknown, "[H]e became incapacitated about 1874 when they moved to Guernsey County, Ohio."[75] Tom and his wife Dorcas (*nee* Neely) Cheadle raised a family of four: Elizabeth (1847-1924), Anna M. (1856-1936), William Dean (1860-1949), and Florence Nightingale (1863-1943).

Thomas Dinsmore Cheadle died January 16, 1903, and is buried in Northwood Cemetery in Cambridge, Ohio. His widow Dorcas (1825–1904) died a year later at Moundsville, West Virginia. She is buried by his side at Cambridge, Ohio.

Their son, William "Willie" Dean Cheadle, was also a tailor in West Virginia, Kentucky, and Ohio. He eventually settled at Utica, Ohio, in 1906, where he owned a print shop and tailor business. He died December 9, 1949, age 90, at Mount Vernon, Ohio, but is buried in Mount Rose Cemetery in Moundsville, West Virginia—which makes me feel very old. Why? I, too, was born in Stockport and, at the time of "Willie" D. Cheadle's funeral in 1949, I was living in Stockport, age one.[76]

---

[75] Williston, *op. cit.*, p. 81.
[76] Doctor Asia H. Whitacre (1898-1993) of Chesterhill came to Stockport to conduct the rites of passage.

Questions Number 18 and Number 19:

Who Gave Windsor Township Its Name? Who Gave Stockport Its Name?

Cheadle genealogists assert, "John Cheadle came from Windsor, Vt., and gave the name of Windsor to Windsor township and Windsor town, afterwards changed to Stockport." But the first postmaster, Samuel Beswick, was forced to choose a different name because "Windsor" was already in use in Ohio. So Beswick submitted the name of his own home town—Stockport, England.

The first post office at Stockport was in the Beswick brothers' dry goods store (now razed) in 1838, located between the present-day four-story Lodge Hall and the site of the bygone beauty salon/barbershop. When the Stockport Sesquicentennial Committee published *Stockport, Ohio—A Compendium of Historical Information* in 1984, Keith Walker, the author's brother, donated a copy to the Public Library in Stockport, England.

Samuel Beswick's brother—James—left Stockport and moved to Van Buren County, Iowa. There, in 1849 he made a small financial donation to have a nearby railroad station built provided it be named "Stockport."[77] But why was "Windsor" chosen? The Cheadle brothers were from Windsor, Vermont, which was named for Windsor, Connecticut, which was named for the town of Windsor in Berkshire on the River Thames in England. Take your choice.

YOUR NOTES

---
[77] Walker, *Stockport, Ohio: A Compendium of Historical Information*, 1984, p. 111.

Question Number 20

Why Has Stockport Survived?

The Terrace Theory

It was never certain that Stockport, Ohio, would survive to 2024. The post office at Big Bottom continued only five years, 1833 to 1838; at Brokaw 40 years, 1898 to 1938; at Roxbury 83 years, 1855 to 1938; at Hooksburg 42 years, 1872 to 1914; but at Stockport from January 26, 1838, to the present—185+ years.

Unlike other settlements at river's edge, the terrace at Stockport prevents widespread flooding and destruction. In turn, the dam and lock #6 (built at Stockport 1837-43) paused steamboats and other river traffic, powered grain and sawmills (the first in 1842), then powered an electric turbine and the village's first electrical grid, followed by the development of salt wells, oil wells, an oil refinery, doctors, dentists, saloons, blacksmith shops, stage coach stop, grain mills, a ferry, hotels, a bridge, telegraph, railroad, drugstores, telephone switchboard, churches, schools, lodge halls, theaters, two newspapers,[78] restaurants, hotels, apartments, and even a horse-drawn taxi service to Pennsville and back—all of which created a shipping, receiving, and transfer point for merchants, farmers, and travelers from Pennsville, Chesterhill, and communities at Dale, Todds, Roxbury, and East Windsor.

Malta landed the first major manufacturing corporations and McConnelsville landed the county seat, courts, and, importantly, the shortcut route over the ridges then down to Olive Green Creek, then Beverly, Coal Run, Lowell, and Marietta. Whereas the steamboat had put Stockport in the transportation and commercial loop between Pittsburgh and Zanesville, the automobile and highway era via the shortcut from McConnelsville over ridges to Hackney bypasses it.

---

[78] *The Coopperhead Ventilator* and *The Stockport Times*.

Also in support of the terrace theory, contrast the fate of the hamlet of Big Rock. On January 18, 1838, Asa Emerson recorded a plat of the town of Big Rock on Lot #49 on the river bottom opposite Luke Chute dam (near the former Graham farm). The plat contained 13 house lots, each five by ten poles. In the 1840 U.S. Census, Big Rock was home to ten families with a population of 61. But it lasted less than ten years. On December 23, 1847, the Muskingum River flooded, cut a channel around the end of Luke Chute dam, and swept the hamlet of Big Rock off the map.[79] In 1993, according to gravel company heavy equipment operator Richard Kern of Stockport, commercial gravel excavations unearthed a few remnants of Big Rock, such as stones and curbstones used to construct water wells, presumably where houses had stood.[80]

Thus, in the immediate wake of the 1913 flood the vast majority of structures and dwellings at Stockport remained high and dry.[81] Rather than seeking aid, most of the citizens at Stockport collected money and goods and sent them to downriver victims from Roxbury to Marietta, virtually all of whom suffered unprecedented devastation and hardships.

---

[79] Nearly a hundred years later, from the mid-1920s to early 1940s, the area opposite Luke Chute dam and locks was known as The Boy Scout Farm and was under the aegis of the Southeastern Ohio Boy Scout Council. Marietta businessman Orton C. Dunn (c. 1785-8/30/1933) was its moving spirit. He had enjoyed the site as a lad, thus, after his success in the oil and gas business, he bought the land for a boy scout reservation and named it Endubonah, which means "Big Chief." The camp was one of only two in Morgan County. The other scout camp was at Nixon Grove in Deerfield Township. For more on the activities and leadership of Orton Dunn of Marietta and his commitment to boy scouting, see Appendix E. His death notice appeared in the *Morgan County Democrat*, August 30, 1933, p. 1.
[80] Walker, *Stockport, Ohio: A Compendium of Historical Information*, 1984, p. 111.
[81] Folklore at Stockport holds that the high-water mark of the 1913 flood on Main Street was the first stone step on the lower (i.e. river side) of the front porch of Judge Riecker's rental duplex house (where Helen Mills and Grace Walker used to live). The floodwaters never reached the first floor of the house itself. Another tradition says the high-water mark was six inches above the eaves of the railroad station. Although the station was razed long ago, the two folklores, along with numerous photographs along the river front, are reasonably consistent. Fortunately, the vast majority of Stockport, its residents, and structures remained "high and dry."

Questions Number 21 and Number 22:

What Is the Earliest Date on a Tombstone in the Stockport Cemetery?
What is the Oldest Known Tombstone in Morgan County, Ohio?

On July 23, 1942, C. B. Ray, Stockport correspondent for the *Morgan County Democrat*, stated in his weekly column, "Facts and Folks of Windsor":

> …let us tell you that the earliest date we have found in the Stockport Cemetery, is 1812. The cemetery has been enlarged. Homer Lane, the caretaker and sexton, is keeping it in first class condition. At this time lots are sold and a record kept of all burials. Later we hope to tell you how many are buried here, on all marked and discernible graves.

Whether "1812" referred to the person's date of birth or death, Ray did not say, nor did he follow up later with a story, name, or list. Thus, he or she, who was born or died in 1812 and cited by Ray 130 years later, remains unknown. What a pity Ray mentioned a date but not the person's name, age, etc. The oldest date on a gravestone in the Stockport Cemetery, when all of the graves in Windsor Township and all nearby cemeteries were catalogued in 1979, was that of Esther Carter (1807–1841), born in England, the wife of James and mother of William H. Carter (1841-1926). However, its numerals were badly worn, thus those years may be inaccurate. Per the Internet, Esther was the wife of James [1810-????] and mother of William H. Carter (1841-1926)[82], who was born at Stockport. There were also a few other graves from the 1840s, but none with a legible date-of-death pre-dating Nathan Sidwell, Jr.'s 1834 plat of the village. Apparently, Stockport came first, then established its graveyard.

---

[82] Maggie Guttermuth of Akron, Ohio, helped catalogue all 32 cemeteries. See Richard Walker and Maggie Guttermuth, *Here Lies a Complete List of Tombstone Inscriptions of Windsor Township, Morgan County, Ohio, and All Nearby Cemeteries*, May, 1979.

The oldest known tombstone in Morgan County is in Windsor Township. In 1979 Richard Barrett and I found a very well-preserved sandstone marker, face-down, along the south side of Windsor TR39 on his late father John's farm, between Roxbury and Brokaw. It is the only remaining stone from the Nott Cemetery:

In Memory of

POLLY SAMPSON

who died on the fourth day of Octob

er, Anno Domni 1805

aged 27 years

The tombstone is in excellent condition—even the poetic verse in small print is legible. Locals say the township road crew threw the tombstones aside in order to put the road from Roxbury to Brokaw through. For nearly fifty years I have tried to determine Polly's identity. For example, not a single Ohio Company executive, official, or settler was named Sampson. As well, who, where, when, and how did someone make such a beautiful, artful sandstone grave marker in 1805?[83] For historical preservation, Barrett's mother, the late Virginia (*nee* Ross) Barrett (1918-2006), donated the tombstone to the Morgan County Historical Society in 1994.

---

[83] In 2023 Marietta College Librarian Linda Showalter suggested a theory: Could the stonemason have been Big Bottom settler James Patten, whom Indians had captured January 1, 1791, at Big Bottom? Patten, held captive for *four years*, was presumed by Marietta officials and his relatives in New England to be dead. But prior to the Treaty of Greeneville in 1795, at a nine-for-nine prisoner swap with tribes in northwest Ohio, he was discovered and freed. Having no means of support, after the Treaty he stayed in southwestern Ohio, doing contract work for the Army. He later returned to Marietta where, as part of its final settlement with stockholders, the Ohio Company granted him (as it had all *bona fide* settlers and stockholders) 100-acre Lot #40 in Range 11, Township 8, in Big Bottom Allotment. (See map, p. 29.) Patten, however, sold it and eventually lived at Belpre where he was a stonemason. I have read Patten's personal letters to family and friends in New England written after his return to the Muskingum (housed at the Clements Library in Ann Arbor, Michigan). What a surprise! On the one hand, Patten's spelling was so atrocious it was difficult to discern even his two-letter words. Clearly, he had had little formal education; *on the other hand, his penmanship was consistently the most beautiful I have ever seen!* Could it be, Showalter asks, that stonemason Patten at Belpre carved the beautiful Polly Sampson tombstone in 1805 (found on the Richard Barrett farm near Brokaw in 1979, lone remnant of the Nott Cemetery)? Even the short verse in small print is legible! (A photograph of Polly Sampson's remarkable tombstone is in Walker, *Wolf Creek and the Muskingum*, 1996, opposite page 343.)

Questions Number 23 and Number 24

What Is Mother Nott's Hole? Where Is Mother Nott's Hole?

Windsor Township men familiar with the river and its history claim that Mother Nott's Hole was the deepest spot in the Muskingum River. It was well-known to Muskingum keelboat crews in the pre-dam (i.e., pre-slackwater, pre-1850) era who poled their boats and barges up and down the river canal-style.[84]

First came canoes, then rafts, then large flatboats, then pirogues, then keelboats, then steamboats. Keelboats employed three or four men, each with a long pole who, on the captain's command, walked in tandem on both sides of the boat simultaneously, pushing back against their long poles, pushing the boat against the current with their arm, back, and leg muscles:

> The keel-boats were constructed much after the fashion of a canal-boat . . . handsomely trimmed and painted, and having a "race-board" on each side for the crew to walk on in pushing. These race-boards were supported by rows of "knees," which were pieces of timber sawn or hewn from a stump, forming right angles. They were firmly pinned to the sides of the craft, and afforded a strong basis not only for the crew, but also for barrels and other heavy freight to be tumbled about on. The regular crew was six men and a captain. On the ponds all the crew set their poles at once; but in ascending ripples, they had to "break hands," as it was termed. The captain (always at the helm) would cry out "Up at the head!" when the two nearest the bow would go forward and set. Then he would cry out again "Seconds, two!" when the two next would go up. Then "Up behind!" when the two nearest the stern would go up and set. In this way there would always be at least two poles set so that the boat could not get the advantage of them.[85]

---

[84] See Appendix D. p. 91.
[85] Williams, *History of Washington County, Ohio*, 1881, pp. 538-39; Walker, *Stockport, Ohio*, p. 66.

Before the dams were built the Muskingum River was seldom very deep. Indeed, accounts at pre-Stockport in the first third of the 1800s, such as Walter Newton's reminiscences, note that the practice of wading across the river was quite common.[86] However, a few places year-round were exceptionally deep. According to oral tradition at Stockport, Mother Nott's Hole was the deepest natural spot in the Muskingum. (See quote on p. 66.) Those who swam in the river in the 1950s assert that it was at least 40+ feet deep. Its location may be determined three ways:

1) Mill Run flows virtually due south, the mouth of which empties into the Muskingum about 306 yards upriver (i.e. due south) from Mother Nott's Hole and about 370 yards upriver from Hidden Spring, all south of relocated SR266. Mother Nott's Hole is approximately 20 feet south of (i.e., out from) the northernmost point where the Muskingum River suddenly bends southeastward.[87] One may speculate that, for tens of thousands of years, the due-north current rammed the north bank at the sharp curve, roiling the river bottom, eventually creating a deep crevice–or hole–about 20 feet out from the present-day (2024) northern edge of the river.

2) The GPS coordinates of Mother Nott's Hole are: **39°, 32', 18.66" N; 81°, 44', 35.67' W**. Normal river surface at the site is about 629 feet above sea level.[88]

3) See location plots on the Google Earth photograph on page 63.

Stories regarding Mother Nott's Hole circulated at Stockport for decades. For example, about 1959 a woman camper from afar drove upriver to Stockport seeking the help of any local young man reputed to be a good swimmer. She said she and her husband had rented a cabin down the river, she had arrived first, and

---
[86] Walker, *Stockport, Ohio*, 1984, pp. 62-3.
[87] By car, the landmarks are a short distance upriver from the general vicinity of Point Lookout, the intersection of CR36/SR266, and site of the old Boy Scout Farm. Luke Chute dam is below the next big bend down the river.
[88] Goggle Earth, 2022.

he was to join her later; that, to unload her station wagon, she had parked it on the bank with the back of the vehicle toward the river and, when she opened the hatch-back, her bowling ball suddenly rolled out of the back of the station wagon, down the bank, and disappeared into the river. Thus, "would any good swimmer in Stockport, for a good fee, be willing to recover the ball from the bottom of the river?" But when she described where their cabin was located, there were no takers.[89] One may presume, with a high degree of confidence, her bowling ball is still, so to speak, in the gutter.

Little recent information on Mother Nott's Hole has circulated. However, avid boater Russell Tippett of Burr Oak and his son, using an underwater radar-equipped boat, reported circa 1985 that the hole appeared to be "mostly filled with tree limbs and debris."

Among early keelboatmen noted at Zanesville:

> John Carpenter had the keelboat "Retuna," afterward named the "Little Toin." His trade was from Zanesville to Pittsburgh, also he was the owner of other boats in the Cincinnati and Kanawha trade … in 1820 and 1825. Victor Stull and his brother Harry, the father and uncle of Captain Stull, of Beverly; Lemuel Swift, afterward a prominent steamboat pilot; Captain Birch, of Marietta, who was on the river piloting steamboats until he was nearly eighty years old. … Dudley Davis of Cat's creek; Tiff and Ross Nott [brothers from Roxbury]; Ab and Hark Boyd; [and] Paul, Alexander, and George Hahn were among the most prominent keel-boatmen.[90]

---

[89] Dan Wallace of Roxbury; Keith Walker of Akron; Chet Cunningham of Stockport, 2021-23.
[90] *Biographical and Historical Memoirs of Muskingum County, Ohio*, 1892, p. 93. Punctuation added for clarity. The satellite image on p. 63 is courtesy of Google Earth. See also Appendices D and K.

Sooner or later, as described above, a member of the boat crew, poling a craft loaded with goods to market up the Muskingum at Zanesville or downriver to Marietta, Parkersburg, Cincinnati, Louisville, or beyond, perchance stuck his pole down Mother Nott's Hole, snapping it in two, suddenly pitching him and sometimes fellow crewmen into the river, which forced the captain to tie-up along the bank and seek local help in rescuing those pitched overboard and, if need be, recover drifting cargo, frantic animals, not to mention cursing men. The shouting, swearing, turmoil, and chaos alerted, and often alarmed, nearby residents along both sides of the river, who then rushed to help save all the men, animals, cargo, equipment, barrels, etc., they could.

In 1845 two families were clearly within earshot of such shouting, turmoil, and tragedy. 1. Atop the river bank directly south across the river from Mother Nott's Hole stood the nearest farmhouse—that of S. M. Evans. 2. Seven-tenths of a mile directly upriver from S. M. Evans' house, also on the Roxbury side, was Asa Cheadle's house, referred to elsewhere.[91][92]

Another well-known location along the southwest shore of the Muskingum River, where Rev. John Heckewelder made an overnight rest stop in 1773, was the Big Rock. Heckewelder said the rock was 70 feet long, 25 feet high, and 22 feet wide. The O.& L.K.R.R. dynamited the rock in 1886-87.

---

[91] Unfortunately farm owners and residents north of the Muskingum River in that region are not shown on William D. Emerson's *Map of Roxbury Township* in 1845 because the river at that time and place was the north boundary of Washington County. "S. M. Evans" was Samuel M. Evans. He wed Polly White, both of Roxbury Township, Washington County, Ohio, on August 29, 1825. Notable Asa Cheadle, Justice of the Peace, eldest of the Muskingum Valley Cheadles who arrived from Vermont in 1799 and/or 1800, wed Sally Divens of Roxbury Township on August 22, 1816, one of his three wives. His first wife was Mercey Hersey, whom he wed January 20, 1802, in the Northwest Territory (i.e., before Ohio statehood). [Bernice Graham and Elizabeth S. Cottle, *Washington County, Ohio, Marriages, 1789–1840*, 1976, p. 99.] N.B. Phoebe (*nee* Kent) wed Tiffin G. Nott on Christmas Day, 1827. After Tiffin died, she married Tiffin's brother, Stewart M. Nott, on November 1, 1832. (N.B. Contrary to genealogical postings on the Internet, Simeon Nott died in Ohio **in 1825**, not 1835. The source of the confusion, as Marietta College scholar and research librarian Linda Showalter discovered, is the fact he was referred to by name in a court land action in Marietta *ten years after he died*, giving a false impression to present-day genealogists and researchers he was still living in 1835.)

William Emerson, "Map of Roxbury Township," *Washington County, Ohio*, 1845, p. 10, reprinted in 1976, is on p. 66. For relative distances, see Google Earth photo on p. 67.

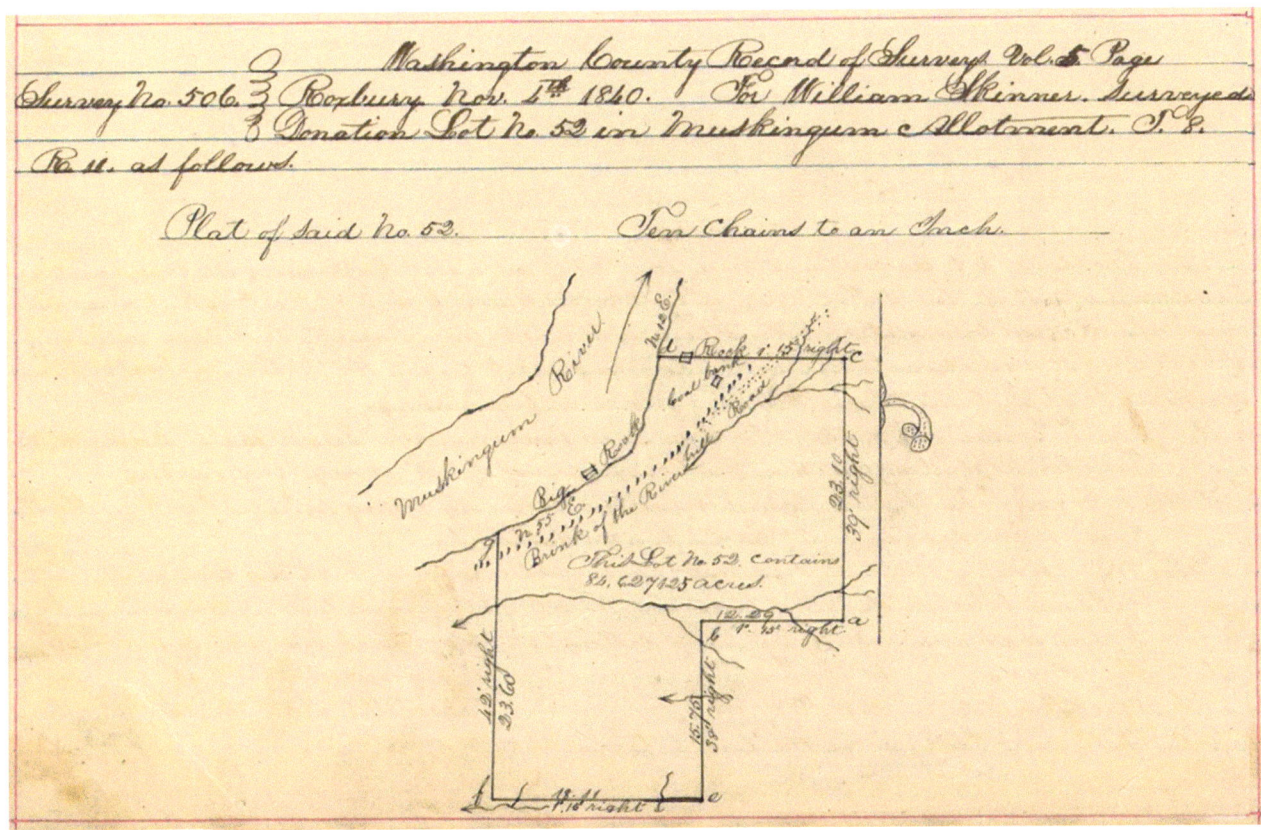

Washington County, Ohio, Record of Survey Number 506 of Survey Vol. 5, Roxbury Nov. 4, 1840. For William Skinnner. Surveyed Donation Lot No. 52 in Muskingum Allotment T. 8. R. 11 as follows: Plat of said No. 52. Ten Chains to an Inch. [See **"Big # Rock"** on the River's SW shore.] For unknown reasons Skinner added, "This Lot No. 52 contains 84.627425 acres." Unlike Rev. John Heckewelder's overnight rest stop at the Big Rock in 1773 with boatloads of Indian converts headed upstream, some of whom went to hunt buffalo on Wolf Creek, by 1840 all local buffalo had vanished from the area. Heckewelder noted the rock was 70 feet long, 25 feet high, and 22 feet wide. The O.&L.K. R.R. dynamited the Big Rock in 1886-87 to lay track through Roxbury. For the Indians the Big Rock had served as the eastern terminus of a trail to and from western villages on the Scioto River and beyond.

YOUR NOTES

Question Number 25

Who Was Mother Nott?

An article in the *Morgan County Herald* many decades ago, date unknown, states:

THE DEEPEST PLACE IN THE MUSKINGUM RIVER

> Where is the deepest water in the Muskingum River? According to Frank Blackmer [1884-1979], the water at 'Mother Nott's hole' on the Muskingum, just above Hidden Spring, enjoys that distinction, with a depth of seventy feet. According to our informant, the spot derived its name from a pioneer settler at that point named Mother Nott, who, upon the approach of a flatboat, would rush to the river and wave the flat-boatmen to the other side, where they could use the poles by which they were powering the boat.[93]

In 2022 Chester "Chet" Cunningham, a native of the Roxbury-Brokaw area, speculated that the previous owner of the S. M. Evans farm and house shown on the 1845 map of Roxbury Township on the south bank of the river directly across from the north bend in the Muskingum and Mother Nott's Hole, had been a Nott family. [See "S. M. Evans" house location in 1845 on the map on page 67.]

Mother Nott had firsthand knowledge of the boat accidents, delays, injuries to crewmen, costs, chaos, and unholy cursing caused by the hole across the river from her house. Thus, when she heard a boat approaching, she hurried to river bank, calling to the crewmen and captain to beware of the deep hole in the river bottom at the north bend. No doubt her fame spread rapidly up and down the Muskingum as captains and crews (which sometimes included her sons, Tiff and Ross, who lived at Zanesville) alerted others to "Beware of Mother Nott's Hole."

---

[93] *Morgan County Herald*, n.d., quoted in Mary Frances Irene Evans, "Evans Family Genealogical MSS., 1964," courtesy of Richard Martin via Chet Cunningham of Stockport, Ohio, 2023.

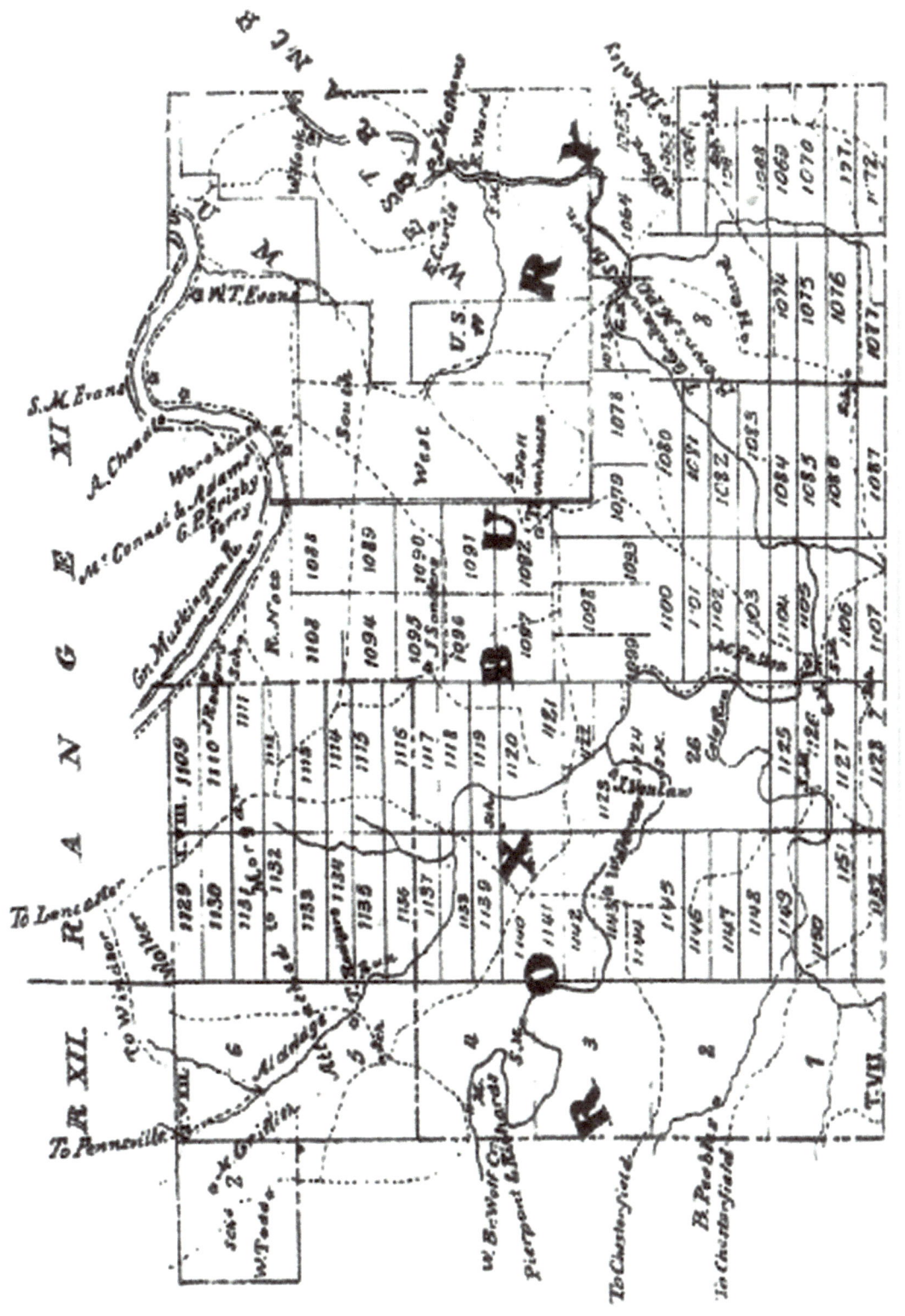

Roxbury Township, Washington County, Ohio
William D. Emerson
-- 1845 --

Cunningham was wiser than he knew—a widow's dower! Research in 2022 by astute, indefatigable scholar Marietta College Research Librarian Linda Showalter, who has ". . . a keen interest in uncovering the history of local women," has narrowed the mystery of Mother Nott's identity:

> Which Phoebe Nott [are you] referring to? There was Phoebe Kent Nott, wife of Tiffin and [later] Stewart, and there was Phoebe Richmond Nott, wife of James. . . . Experience foretells that her identity will be revealed shortly after the publication of your booklet.[94]
>
> Simeon Nott [1775-1825] was the owner of Lots 40,[95] 41, and part of 42 in Range 11, Township 8, Big Bottom (a.k.a. Muskingum) Allotment, from 1799 until his death in 1825. Simeon's widow Mary ("Polly") Nott, along with his children, owned it from the time of his death until it was sold to Samuel M. Evans, William J. Evans, and Simeon Evans, Jr., in 1836. Mary ("Polly") Nott retained a widow's dower of 25 acres on the North end of lots 40 and 41, even after the land was sold. Therefore, it seems to me that Mary ("Polly") Nott is the most likely candidate for the title, "Mother Nott." Of course, we do not know the precise living situations of the Nott women during this time period, so it is possible that one of her daughters-in-law, such as Phebe Kent Nott, was also present on this land and could have been "Mother Nott." My vote is with Mary "Polly," as she was the mother of this family of Nott's, including sons, "Tiff and Ross Nott . . . [who lived at Zanesville and] were among the most prominent keelboatmen on the Muskingum.[96]

Mother Nott's compassionate shouts and alarms, one may assume, were not only motivated for the safety of her sons Tiffin "Tiff" G. Nott (1799–1831) and Rosewell "Ross" H. Nott (1805–1854), and their fellow crewmen, but extended to other

---

[94] Linda Showalter, Marietta College, Email, December 1, 2022.
[95] "The first recorded owner of Lot #40 is Col. Alexander Oliver of Belpre who sold it to Simeon Nott in 1799. Source: "James Patten Honored Today in Belpre," Phillip L. Crane, *The Marietta Times*, September 26, 2015. James Patten was the only white captive taken hostage by the Indians at the Big Bottom Massacre who returned to the Ohio Company and Muskingum Valley to live.
[96] Linda Showalter, Marietta College, Email, December 9, 2022, and subsequent correspondence.

crews as well. Hopefully readers can provide information regarding this remarkable pre-Stockport era woman whose name the Muskingum Valley has almost, but not yet, lost and forgotten:[97] **Mary "Polly" Nott (1775-1835)**.

Yet, despite extensive genealogical research, her maiden name remains uncertain!

I think she was Mary Polly (*nee* **Peyton**) Nott as stated on Family Search. Why? Her son's middle name was "Paton"!

But various genealogical anomalies arise, creating uncertainty, thus calling for caution and better evidence of the identity of this remarkable lady.[98] One source states she was born in New England, moved to Kentucky, then married in Cincinnati. But two obstacles block the path to her identity: 1. The Hamilton County courthouse in Cincinnati burned down three times, destroying early marriage records. 2. When Windsor Township, Morgan County, Ohio, cut the first road from Roxbury to Brokaw, the road crew destroyed the Nott Cemetery, which was located on the present-day [2024] Richard Barrett farm. No list of names of those buried there is known to exist.

---

[97] The eight children of Simeon Nott, Sr. (1770-1825) and Mary "Polly" (*nee* Peyton) Nott (1775-1835) were: 1. Simeon P. Nott (1795-1827), 2. John Craven Nott (1797-1818), 3. Phelinda Nott (died 1797), 4. Tiffen G. Nott (1799-1831), 5. Roswell H. Nott (1805-1854), 6. Stewart Massena Nott (1811-1868), 7. Samuel Beeman Nott (1814-1855), and their youngest, 8. Henry Paton Nott (1818-1874), who wed Margaret Elizabeth Hiler in Roxbury Township in Washington County, Ohio, on October 30, 1844, and issued 11 children. One source indicates that Mother Nott was born in Ross Township, Butler County, Ohio, far north of Cincinnati and Hamilton County. Regarding Nott keelboatmen on the Muskingum: "Dudley Davis of Cat's creek, Tiff and Ross Nott [Henry Nott's older brothers by almost 20 years!], Ab and Hark Boyd, Paul Alexander and George Hahn were among the most prominent keel-boatmen [on the Muskingum]." (*Biographical and Historical Memoirs of Muskingum County*, 1892, p. 93. Courtesy of Linda Showalter). For the record (which does not appear in Bernice Graham and Elizabeth S. Cottle, *Washington County, Ohio, Marriages 1789-1840*, published in 1976) their youngest child of eight, son Henry **Paton** Nott, and Margaret Elizabeth Hiler were wed on October 30, 1844, in Roxbury Township, Washington County, Ohio, by, Isaac Baker, JP. Henry and Margaret had eleven children: 1. Perrin Rosewell Nott (1844-1923); 2. Philinda Beggs Nott (1846-1919); 3. William Alexander Nott (1849-1926); 4. Amanda E. Nott (1850-1930); 5. Willis Marion Nott (1851-1854); 6. Rachael A. Nott (1854-1919); 7. Harriet Nott (1855-1867); 8. Rhoda E. Nott (1856-1942); 9. Lucetta Susan Nott (1859-1935); 10. Laura A. Nott (1861-1935); and 11. William Alonzo Nott (1863-1923). [Family Search]
[98] My address: Richard Walker, Ph.D., 4210 Trilithon Court, West Lafayette, IN 47906.

Questions Number 26 and Number 27:

What Was One of the Most Lamented Tragedies in the pre-Stockport Era? Who Described It in Both Graphic and Poetic Detail in 1837?

Setting aside the Indian massacre of twelve Ohio Company settlers at Big Bottom in 1791, Dr. Charles Robertson, in *History of Morgan County, Ohio* in 1886, summarizes the basic facts. Then, in conclusion, we will go back half a century more to 1837 and let Rial Cheadle present specific details and his erudite tribute.

Robertson gives this account of what early pioneers called "a circle hunt":

> At a wolf-hunt in 1822 [sic, 1825] a young man named Joel Sherman was accidentally shot near the headwaters of Mill Run. The hunters became demoralized through the free use of whisk[e]y, and neglected to act upon any concerted plan. Several of them, seeing a deer in a hollow, began firing at it. Levi Davis and P. J. Patterson, who were of the party, thinking themselves in the way of the bullets, hid under a log. The firing ceased, when [Joel] Sherman was discovered to have been shot through the body. He was taken to the house of John Henery, where he died after suffering for several days.[99]

Young Sherman was taken to and eventually died at John Henery's farm house, (not far downriver from Hooksburg, the easternmost acreage of which still feeds the headwaters of Mill Run, which, flowing due south, empties into the Muskingum about 370 yards upriver from Hidden Spring and about 306 yards upriver from Mother Nott's Hole, both in the general vicinity of Point Lookout (CR36/SR266). [See Google Earth image, p. 63.][100] The articulate, poetic, and heroic Rial Cheadle graphically, then poetically, described the tragic details. The original printed document bears his name, followed by "February 15, 1837, Morgan County, Ohio." Verbatim:

---

[99] N.B. Robertson, *History of Morgan County, Ohio*, 1886, p. 399. Robertson states the hunt occurred in 1822. That is an error. It was in 1825. The headwaters of Mill Run are the fields and gullies behind the hamlet of Hooksburg. Mill Run flows due south to the Muskingum.
[100] Young Paddock Cheadle built and operated a "corn cracker" mill and a sawmill on Mill Creek in pioneer days. Charles Robertson, *History of Morgan County, Ohio*, 1886, p. 407.

In Memory of Joel Sherman,

WHO DEPARTED THIS LIFE, JAN. 3d, 1825, AGED 22 YEARS

The circumstances attending the death of this young man were truly affecting. Four days previous to his death, a large number of young persons met in Windsor, about nine miles south east of M'Connelsville, for the purpose of a Wolf hunt. Many of them came from Waterford, amongst whom was this unfortunate man. He, through the kind attention of his parents, was previously restored from a long and severe illness, and by them he was warned of his danger, but all to no purpose. He went as if the Enchanter led him on, never to return. He arrived on the ground, proceeded on the line of march; the promiscuous group encircled the forest. Many were thrown into a narrow defile leading down a creek; a deer came running through the crowd—a general firing soon took place—all was disorder and dismay—the implements of death made a dismal roar,—Young SHERMAN was mortally wounded—a ball passed through his shoulder, and lodged near the vitals. He put his hand to his shoulder; saw the deep stained crimson; he told his father he was wounded—a distressing groan was heard with the long faltering voice of supplication. He fainted; the paleness of death sat on his countenance. They conveyed him in agony to a habitation; all just means were used for his recovery, but to no purpose. Meantime his mother and sister came to console him. To the former he spoke with much thankfulness, to the latter with all the affection of a brother. His bosom heaved with tenderness, and all his words were of love. No common objects did his thoughts control; he spoke as mortal near the grave. He bid all prepare for death. Near his last he asked for a drink, took the glass in his hand, returned it to his friend, and ere the eye turned to behold him, immediately expired. He is now consigned to the narrow limits of the grave, forever released from the dull cares of Mortality.

Rial Cheadle's poetic tribute written in 1837:

> I pray thee to teach me the long notes of sadness,
> And speak of my brother that sleeps with the dead,
> Who oft as he met me, spake smiling with gladness,
> But now in lone silence he pillows his head,
> He never returns to behold his near kindred,
> It seems he's forgotten to visit again,
> O what is the reason his spirit is hindred,
> That he should in silence forever remain.
>
> The lone shade of evening this thought may resemble,
> When twilight is ending, we shiver afraid,
> Our thoughts do pursue thee, we ponder and tremble,
> We view thee before us, again thou dos't fade,
> How oft in the vision of sleep we do trace thee,
> And see every feature that nature could show,
> Then blest by thy converse, a moment we face thee,
> And words of soft pleasure in symphony flow.
>
> Thou once didst recover from long lingering illness,
> Health sprang in thy bosom and night turn'd to day,
> Thy spirit was bless'd with composure and stillness,
> Thy sister did greet thee so cheerful and gay.
> But now we do mourn thee, 'tis all melancholy,
> Thy youth was so ruddy, so blooming and fair,
> Our hopes are now cut off, to finish our folly,
> We're press'd down with sorrow and burthen'd with care.
>
> Alas! 'twas in vain that thy kindred entreated,
> Their mild admonitions prov'd useless and vain,

That firm resolution so warmly was heated,
He fled from our presence and quickly was slain,
Alas! what disaster that moment assail'd him,
The grim roar of death made a breach in the crowd,
He groan'd, in an instant his strength quickly fail'd him,
The guns of the forest were clashing and loud.

His hand was expanded and laid on his shoulder,
He soon saw the token of terror and pains,
The signs of his visage grew paler and colder,
And strange was the tremor that passed through his reigns.
He spake with assurance, now death is my portion,
And then to his father, distress'd did call,
The crowd then was struck with dreadful commotion,
The chase was soon over and gloomy the pall.

His father astonish'd drew near to behold him,
He ran in compassion to where he did lie,
The stranger look'd fearful to hear what was told him,
A tender emotion did start in his eye.
He bid all farewell so excessively bleeding,
The main spring of life from its fountain did pour,
Then with the Jehovah his spirit was pleading,
To favor and pardon the sinner once more.

He pray'd from his soul with a fervent devotion,
At thoughts of Eternity drawing so near,
His countenance glow'd with a solemn emotion,
His looks were expressive and awful sincere,
He liv'd a few days but did never recover,
His friends came to view him with all who were dear,

The greatest of thanks he return'd to his mother,
Who came in such haste, as his end was so near.

He saith now my mother you've come once unto me,
And the sad tidings, I never can live,
Although I anguish, with pleasure I view thee,
'Tis the last act of kindness you ever can give,
And you my companions who weep and condole me,
The scene is now trying most keen and severe,
O never forget me, though time may console ye,
'Tis the last words of JOEL you ever shall hear.

O now be advis'd, hear the words of the dying,
My brother, my sister, your state I deplore,
Ye sorrow to lose me, which causes your sighing,
Prepare now to follow, I'll soon be no more.
He thirsted, they gave him refreshment of water,
He then did receive, took the glass in his hand,
His spirit was quickly releas'd from all torture,
His life blood in motion no longer could stand.

RIAL CHEADLE *Morgan County, Ohio, Feb. 15, 1837*[101]

---

[101] Reprinted by William Dinsmore Cheadle of Utica, Ohio, February 15, 1924, and cited in the *Morgan County Democrat*, July 24, 1924, p. 8. N.B. Cheadle's poem is on the Internet at the University of Rhode Island at Kingston. –RW

Question Number 28:

What Is Now Known Regarding Young Joel Sherman?

Joel Sherman's modest grave in the Waterford Cemetery:

"1803–January 3–1825."

Joel Sherman was a grandson of early Muskingum pioneer farmer Abel Sherman on Sherman's Run, which empties into the Muskingum River two miles north of Beverly, Ohio. Abel, age 50, was killed there on his farm on August 15, 1794, during an Indian raid. Allegedly the Shawnee Silverheels, who kept his campfires near the mouth of Bald Eagle Creek in the pre-Stockport era, was among the attackers. After the Indian war was over, Silverheels was murdered in revenge at the mouth of Bald Eagle Crrek near Stockport by one of Abel Sherman's sons. [See Questions 14 and 16.] Sherman also has a memorial marker in Round Bottom Cemetery near Coal Run.

Silverheels has a memorial marker in the Stockport Cemetery.

YOUR NOTES

Question Number 29

Will I Ever Come to My Final Comments?

I am proud of Stockport, the crucible of folks such as civil rights champion Rial Cheadle and Windsor High School graduate, Malta doctor, and nationally noted author Dr. James Ball Naylor. And who gave Naylor his chance? Doctor Emmet Gatewood of East Windsor under whom Naylor apprenticed at Gatewood's drugstore (still standing in 2024) on Main Street in Stockport. And who gave East Windsor farm boy Emmet Gatewood his chance? A young friend at Roxbury, whom Gatewood did not identify, who invited Gatewood to Brooklyn in New York City to sit in on medical lectures with him. It took! Gatewood returned to the family farm in northeastern Windsor Township then apprenticed three years under Dr. Hiram J. Noyes at nearby Unionville.

Once established at Stockport, Gatewood (1845-1924) developed the largest medical practice in Morgan County in his era. Day or night, rain or shine, he hitched his horse and buggy and off he would go. He was also a generous benefactor to "the outdoor poor." An example of a long buggy ride—rain or shine—from Stockport is his journal entry April 1, 1877, which finds him attending a patient, Otho Elliott's wife, suffering from double breast cancer, at her home at Elliot's Crossroads.

And when, just north of Stockport, a stone crushed a young Italian gandy-dancer on the new Ohio & Little Kanawha Railroad, whom did they seek? Gatewood, an excellent surgeon, went immediately and administered aid. In many instances in which poor patients ("the outdoor poor") could not pay him, Gatewood simply "Charged it to the dust and let the rain settle it." Gatewood, sold his house and drugstore to Dr. Lyne for $4,200 in January 1892.[102] He then moved to Nashville, TN, where he opened a small medical practice and invested in real estate.

---

[102] Clyde K. Swift, *Manuscript*, "Stockport as Seen in "Muskingum Years," 1983?, p. 5.

GATEWOOD

Born October 11, 1887, in Stockport, O. Graduate of Ohio State University, 1907, A. B., 1910, A. M.; Rush Medical College, 1911. Practice: surgery. Assistant attending surgeon at Presbyterian Hospital, 1918, to date. Instructor in surgery at Rush Medical College, 1917, to date. Assistant in physiology at Ohio State University, 1907-10. Member of American Medical Association and Fellow of American College of Surgeons. Author of numerous contributions to surgical clinics of Chicago, and various articles published from time to time in Journal A. M. A., Illinois Medical Journal, etc. Military Service: First Lieutenant, M. R. C., U. S. A. Residence, Webster Hotel, Chicago.

(Photo by Walinger)
GATEWOOD

LEE CONNEL GATEWOOD

Born March 15, 1889, in Stockport, Ohio. Graduate of Ohio State University, 1907, A. B., A. M., 1909; Sigma Xi (honorary) 1908; Rush Medical College, 1911. Practice: internal medicine. Assistant attending physician, Presbyterian Hospital, 1916 to date. Attending physician, Cook County Hospital, 1920 to date. Associate in medicine at Rush Medical College, 1920 to date. Married Grace Marion Blair, October 6, 1914, at Chicago. Member of American Medical Association, Chicago Society of Internal Medicine, Chicago Institute of Medicine and Chicago Pathological Society; also City Club of Chicago. Military Service: Entered service as Lieutenant, M. C., at Fort Riley, Kan., May, 1917, and discharged as Major; served as instructor in medical officers' training camps to December, 1917. Member of U. S. A. Base Hospital No. 13, overseas May, 1918,-March, 1919. Detached from organization and served as Evacuation Officer, Base Hospital Group, Toul, France, September to November, 1918; also Assistant to Chief Surgeon, Third Army, A. E. F., to January, 1919. Citation for meritorious service as Assistant to Chief Surgeon, Third Army, A. E. F. Residence, 5711 Blackstone Avenue, Chicago.

(Photo by Chambers)
LEE CONNEL GATEWOOD

Dr. Emmet Gatewood's Sons Born at Stockport[103]

---

[103] *History of Medicine and Surgery and Physicians and Surgeons of Chicago,* The Biographical Publishing Corp., Chicago, Illinois, 1922, p. 524 [in archive.org.]. Dr. Emmet Gatewood did not believe it proper that parents name their children, thus he gave his first son no first name.

Dr. Emmet Gatewood died in California and is buried in Mount Olivet Cemetery in East Windsor. Two of his sons—one named "Gatewood" (i.e., no first name) (1887-1939), another, Lee Connel Gatewood (1889-1950), both born near Stockport—became noted doctors and surgeons in Chicago.

Of Gatewood's 17 ledger-size Day Books, spanning 1864-1910, 15 were housed at the Institute of Historical Survey in Las Cruses, New Mexico (soon to close). Unfortunately, they could be viewed only in person. His other two Day Books are available on the Internet. His truculent love-hate relationship with Stockport and its irascible, shady, and criminal characters out to extort him make interesting reading [Ledger for October 1885–March 1893]. Indeed, worthy of a national best seller —and Dr. James Ball Naylor had lived it firsthand — hence his famous novel, *Ralph Marlowe*.

And other good local influences, worthy of mention and more include: Many-time mayor Pete Brannon (1873-1946); "Outstanding Postmaster of Ohio" recipient Frank R. "Hank" Faires (1915-2004) and his businessman brother Wilfred "Woody" (1923-1988); high school principal, teacher, and athletic coach "Heck" Harkins (1921-2004); old Mary "Molly" Justice; merchants Bill and Les Wootton[104]; and many others who helped make the village a more vibrant, if not always a better, place than they found it.

Generational family names include Bebout, Calendine, Wallace, McKibben, McCoy, Porter, Van Fossen, Adams, Medley, Brokaw, Oliver, Hook, Smith, Newton, Ring, Scott, Batchelor, Gage, Williams, James, Roland, Rollison, Ewart, Gilbreath, Lowther, Motz, Morrison, Locke, Eddleblute, Bishop, Lane, McDermott, Mosier, Hoover, Farabee, Ellis, Hindman, Smith, and—of course—Cheadles galore! Remember singer/teacher Belford Pickering Cheadle (1895-1960)? He lived next

---

[104] The Wootton Dry Goods store on Main Street in Stockport was built in 1902 and razed in 2021.

door on Broadway Street. And this list of names is only a sample per my first fifteen years of life in Stockport.[105] [See Appendix I.]

Also note, based on Theresa M. Flaherty's in-depth research and expertise on James Ball Naylor: Local character **John Brooks** was the real "Jep Tucker" in Naylor's not-so-fictional novel, *Ralph Marlowe*, set in Stockport and published in 1901. Brooks, age 87, died at his home in Stockport in February, 1930. The true identity of the characters: "Ralph Marlowe" was, in real life, *James Ball Naylor himself*; "Dr. Ephraim Barwood" in real life was **Dr. Wesley Emmet Gatewood**; salesman "Leonidas Walingford Crider" was in real life Zanesville salesman **Ernest B. Schneider**; the fictional bridge tender, in real life, was **Brady Kean**; "Sweety Jimson," in real life, was **Sweetcake Johnson**; the "McDevitts," in real life were the **McDermotts**; the "Gridleys," in real life, were the **Gormleys**; and the Baldy Drug Company was the **Bailey Drug Company** of Zanesville.

Speaking of the Gormleys, Hugh Gormley's complex saga in Stockport and Glouster in particular and in southeastern Ohio in general in the hayday of the underground coal miners is a biographical challenge waiting to be mined.[106]

---

[105] N.B. "**Columbus C. Cheadle, Jr.**, known to many as Jr. departed his ancestral Cheadle Farm [near Roxbury, Ohio] for his home in Heaven on 7/12/2022. He was born in 1938 to Columbus C. Cheadle, Sr, and Marie (Wolfe) Cheadle. He was preceded in death by his parents, his wife of 55 years, Wilda (Johnson) Cheadle and by two grandsons, Jason and Kyle Wilson. He is survived by a daughter, Barbi Cheadle; a son, Tim Cheadle; a step-daughter, Earline Arnott; and a step-son Kenneth Wilson; four grandchildren, Adrianja (Noah) Albrecht, Caleb Cheadle, Sasha (Josh) Lee, and Chad (Bridget) Wilson; and four great-grandchildren, Kylin, Parker and Aver Lee and Bristol Wilson; 8 cows and his faithful dog, Hank. . . . During the Vietnam War, he served stateside in the Army's 123d Maintenance Division. After being honorably discharged, he continued as a mechanic by building a garage on the family farm and starting his own small business, Cheadle's Garage, until he retired *because the computers took over*." He was widely known in the area as a competent and clever mechanic who was honest, reliable and fair in all that he did. Jr. further served his community as an elected official, Windsor Township Trustee, for more than thirty years. . . . [H]e was an active member of his church serving as an usher, Sunday School Superintendent and Board Member. . . . Many also enjoyed the bounty of his sense of humor and general orneriness. He cared deeply and he will be greatly missed! . . . Graveside services [to be held] at Oakland Cemetery near Stockport." (*Marietta Times*, July 15, 2022) [abridged])

[106] Mary ("Molly") Justice, in her old age, is said to have often remarked, "Back in the late 1800s and early 1900s, whenever there was a meeting or gathering of any kind at Stockport, the next day nobody ever asked if there had been a fistfight—just 'Who fought?'" (Source: Grace L. [*nee* Kirkbride] Walker.)

Question Number 30:

Who Was James B. Johnson?

Any roster of war heroes from Windsor Township, Morgan County, Ohio, should include unsung James B. Johnson (2/26/1842 place unknown–11/7/1931 at Bartlesville, OK). Stockport folks who knew him, whether personally or only by reputation, insist—usually with a big grin or chuckle—that the "B." stood for "Bearskin." Unfortunately, Morgan County, Ohio, does not have birth certificates back to 1842, thus can neither confirm nor refute the "B." stood for "Bearskin."[107]

Bearskin's wife, Clara ("Clarissa" [*nee*] Hoon, 1846-1931), was born in Mercer County, Pennsylvania. She came to Ohio with her parents as a little girl. After Bearskin returned home from the Civil War, they wed August 19, 1866, in Morgan County, Ohio.

He and Clara moved from Ohio to Independence, Kansas, in 1906. Then, about 1923, they moved to Bartlesville, Oklahoma, where they lived their remaining years. They had seven children and were married more than 65 years. James died in Oklahoma 13 days after Clara died.

They are buried in Memorial Park Cemetery at Bartlesville. His modest tombstone is shown on the next page [courtesy of Find-A-Grave]:

---

[107] Courtesy of Jon Rex, Morgan County Ohio Health Department, June 6, 2022. All efforts via the Internet to factually established what the "B." in Johnson's middle name stood for, have thus far failed. Those who have additional information are encouraged to write the author: Richard Walker, 4210 Trilithon Court, West Lafayette, Indiana 47906.

JAMES JOHNSON

1842 — 1931
Co. D, 63rd OH VOL V. INF.

Johnson's death notice in the *Morgan County Democrat* adds remarkable facts:

> An outstanding record of service in the Civil war was made by Mr. Johnson who saw five years service in the 63rd Regiment from Ohio. He was twice wounded in battle and was with [General William Tecumseh] Sherman in the famous march [from Atlanta] to the sea. He maintained his membership in the G.A.R. post at Independence, Kansas.[108]

Personal references to Johnson in Morgan County are rare, such as the one below by Stockport native Dr. James Ball Naylor, whose own father died in the Civil War. Naylor was born in 1860 in a cabin in Penn Township near where the three boundaries of Windsor, Penn, and Marion Townships in Morgan County meet.

---
[108] *Morgan County Democrat*, McConnelsville, Ohio, November 26, 1931, p. 2.

After the war Naylor's sorely impoverished family moved cabin-to-cabin—"sometimes hewn, sometimes round logs," he notes—then relocated farm to town.

In Naylor's early teens, the family lived near, then moved *into* Stockport where he had to scrap his way into peer acceptance as "just one of the boys." Naylor, of small frame but great wit, was greatly inspired by Stockport High School teacher James M. Rusk. In 1876 Rusk took student Naylor on a lunch-hour walk and asked Naylor, of slight build, to think about a career other than farming. Naylor did. A few years after he graduated, Naylor began medical training under Dr. Emmet Gatewood at Stockport, taught at Stockport school for four terms for $1.25 a day, then, after medical school, opened his first medical practice at Stockport in competition with his former mentor Dr. Gatewood. Gatewood was not amused and hard feelings followed.

Years later, after both doctors had left Stockport—Naylor first moved his family and practice to Pennsville, then finally to Malta, and Gatewood moved his family to Nashville, Tennessee—they renewed their friendship. Whenever Gatewood visited Stockport-area friends, his East Windsor relatives, or tended family graves in East Windsor (his little girl is buried there), he stopped by Naylor's office in Malta for long and friendly chats about their good-ole Stockport days.

In Naylor's reminiscences of his rough-and-tumble teenage years at Stockport he mentioned Bearskin Johnson:

> The principal sports, games and pastimes of my youth were: Swimming, fishing, baseball and croquet—in summer; skating, hunting, trapping, [etc.] in winter. . . . "Shooting-matches" were held frequently. Each contestant had his own gun; and it was a long-barreled, muzzle-loading, percussion cap rifle. The prizes, usually, were turkeys. On Newton Ridge, Ab Newton was marksman par excellence; all rivals stood in awe of him and his trusty firearm—"Betsy." It was currently believed that Ab couldn't

shoot his best until he had disposed of a liberal number of libations of hard cider. He was an uncle of ex-Sheriff Newton. In the Stockport neighborhood, "Bearskin" Johnson—father of Charles Johnson, now living at Philo—had a reputation second to none, as a "dead-shot." His keen eyesight, steady nerves and true reckoning seldom failed him. I have seen him "drive center" five or six times in succession, at the distance ordinarily stepped-off. A. H. Matson, "Bub," was one of the crack shots of Penn township; and Harmon Seaman, Jesse Timms, Wash Humphrey, and J. L. Benjamin were among the champions around Malta.[109]

Speaking of Mary "Molly" (*nee* Severance) Justice (1854–1944) at Stockport, consider this remarkable tribute to her at age 88 in July, 1942, by C. B. Ray, "Rolling Correspondent" of the *Morgan County Democrat*:

We have heard many ordained men preach, but we listened to a sermon by Mrs. Mary Justice Sunday evening, which surpassed many that came from college men—men supposed to be learned Bible students. The funny part of it was that she did not know that she was delivering a sermon, and it didn't seem to bother her, that she had a poor audience—only me.[110]

But things are now reversed. You have been the good "student" and I have been the poor "teacher." May others improve, correct, and expand upon these notes on Stockport.

Thank you for persisting to . . .

The End.

---

[109] James Ball Naylor, *Rambling Reminiscences*, 1927, pp. 27-8. Courtesy of Naylor scholar and publisher Theresa M. Flaherty.
[110] C. B. Ray, *Morgan County Democrat*, July 9, 1942, p. 2.

Appendix A

The First White Land Owners of the Pre-Stockport Site[111]

by

Rebecca Faires

Stockport, Ohio

1984

1. Caleb Swan was the first white private owner of the pre-Stockport site, Lot #90. The land was part of Lot "number 90 in Range 11, Township 9, and twenty fifth mile square, being the fifth division in the Ohio Company Share entered in the name of Caleb Swan." The original owner of Lot #89 to the north was John Mercer; the original owner of Lot #91 to the south was Increase M. Scott.
2. Major Thomas Doyle of Cincinnati purchased Lot #90 from Caleb Swan, date and price unknown.
3. Charles Vitice (Vattier) bought Lot #90 for $200 from Major Thomas Doyle of Cincinnati. This was actually an indenture pending until ". . . regular deeds are issued by the Muskingum Company . . . ."
4. James Findlay bought Lot #90, along with another 900-acre tract on Racoon Creek, on May 14, 1807, for $900 from Charles Vattier and his wife Pamela of Cincinnati.
5. Nicholas Longworth of Cincinnati purchased Lot #90. Frederick Eveland bought Lot #90 for $500 from Nicholas Longworth on October 16, 1816.
6. John, Moses, and David Eveland (east to west) each bought about 35 acres in Lots #90 and #91 west of the river from Frederick Eveland in July and August, 1825.
7. [Gap in the record]
8. Paddick [Paddock] Cheadle bought 112 acres for $200 from Luther Dearborn in 1821 [?].
9. Joseph Cheadle bought 56 acres for $500 from [his brother Paddock] Cheadle in 1829.
10. Isaac Williams bought 112 acres for $850 from Joseph Cheadle in 1829.
11. Jesse Sidwell bought 112 acres in R11, T9, S25 for $900 from Isaac Williams in 1831.
12. Nathan Sidwell bought 112 acres in R11, T9, S25 from Jesse Sidwell in 1834 and "laid out the town on his own land in 1834."

---

[111] In chronological order from the first white land owner down to the village plat filed by Nathan Sidwell in 1834. The quote in #12 above is from Robertson, *History of Morgan County, Ohio*, 1886, p. 410. Also in Walker, *Stockport, Ohio*, 1984, pp. 63-5. Note: R=range; T=township; S=section; L=lot.

Appendix B
Record of the Presbyterian Congregation of Windsor [Ohio] 1824-1837[112]

Feb. 16th, 1824.

The congregation of Windsor convened pursuant to publick notice given. After sermon a church was organized, consisting of the following members, received on certificate: Silvanus Newton, Richard Cheadle, Asa Cheadle, George Howard [a.k.a. Harward], Elisha Hand, Mary Patterson, Elenor Howard, Elizabeth Newton, Sally Cheadle, Sally Hand
Richard Cheadle and George Howard were chosen ruling elders of the congregation.

April 18th, 1824

Richard Cheadle and George Howard were ordained ruling elders.

June 24th, 1824

Session met according to appointment. Members present: John Hunt Md [moderator]; Richard Cheadle [and] George Howard: [the three] Elders. Constituted with prayer.
The following persons were admitted to the communion of the church. Viz. on certificate[:] Susannah McMillan, Mary McMillan, Abijah Seely, Jane Seely, John Hamilton, Elizabeth Hamilton, Phyanna Boll, Eliza Robinson, Eunice Godfrey.
On examination: Joseph Che[a]dle, Asa Emerson, Martha Craft[;] Sally, wife of Richard Cheadle, [and] Sally, wife of Joseph Cheadle
Adjourned to meet on Saturday 26th inst. Concluded with prayer.

June 26th, 1824

Session met according to adjournment. Constituted with prayer. Members present: John Hunt md [moderator] Richard Cheadle, George Howard, elders.

---

[112] The document's actual title. I thank Steve Hanson of East Windsor for sharing this pre-Stockport, handwritten church log from 1824-etc. Typed and edited for space and clarity, I have organized the various segments and sections in chronological order. All of my edits and clarifications are indicated by brackets. —Rich Walker   N.B.: One part of the handwritten copy, dated January 1964, includes this preface: "January 1964. This record was among the effects of Henry Wakefield Cheadle and given to him by his father, Reverend Henry Clay Cheadle. The original record is in the possession of my sister, Catherine L. Cheadle, Duluth, Minnesota [.] —[signed] Margaret Cheadle (nee Scheff) Fahy, 4803 Matney Avenue, Long Beach, California 90807."

The following persons were admitted to the communion of the church. Viz:
On certificate: Alexander Moorhead, Catherine Moorhead.
On examination: Martha Cheadle, Patty Lells [Sells?] & Elisabeth Emerson.
Session adjourned. Concluded with prayer.

June 27th, 1824

Baptized Lusence, daughter of Asa and Sally Cheadle; Levena, daughter of Alexander & Susannah McMillan[;] & Mary, daughter of Abijah & Jane Seely.

June 12th, 1825

Baptized Asa Percival [Cheadle,] son of Asa & Sally Cheadle

July 3rd, 1825

Baptized Addison Evertt [White] son of Asa & Cynthia White

August 13th, 1825

Session met according to appointment. Constituted with prayers. Members present: John Hunt, Moderator. Richard Cheadle [and] George Howard [Harward], elders.
Admitted to the communion of the Church. On certificate: Phineas C. Keyes, Mary A. Keyes, Mary H. Cheadle[.]
On examination[:] Edward Richmond, Martha Richmond, Thomas Tuff, Dorothy Tuff. Session adjourned. Concluded with prayer.

April 26th, 1829

Martha Richmond removed [from the church roll] by death.

mid-August 1829

[A man, whose name appeared on a previous page which is missing, violated] the sanctity of the Sabbath by traveling on the river in a canoe and also by being employed in his sugar camp. In relation to these offences he professed repentance and purposes of amendment. Agreeably to a resolution of session, he was for these offences, rebuked and admonished by the Moderator. To which censure he submitted. Resolved that the above minutes be read in the congregation. Session adjourned. Concluded with prayer.

August 17 and 18, 1829

Baptized Joshua and William children of Ebenezer and Elizabeth Robinson. [The next day, the 18th] Dismissed Elizabeth Robinson.

October 9, 1829

John Hamilton removed by death.

December 20, 1829

Baptized Harriett, daughter of George + Elenor Harward

January 17, 1830

Baptized Priscilla and Elizabeth, daughters of Samuel and Eunice Godfrey

February 18, 1835

Dismissed Elizabeth Hamilton

April 2, 1835

Dismissed Phyanna Bole

September 24, 1837

Session met according to appointment, opened with prayer[.] Members present: Bennet Roberts, moderator[;] Martin H. Cheadle, Asa Emerson, Asa White, [the three] Elders. Admitted to the communion of the Church by letter Asa Bailey[,] Harriet Tufts and Susan Hook. On examination Amory Keyes, George Fry, Marian Tufts [pages missing? Next page lists:] Orsemus McVeigh, Joseph McVeigh, Richard McKibben, Sarah (Terah) Smith, John Glen, Elizabeth Glen, Rebecca Nichels, Lucy Lawrence, Jane Smith, Jane McVeigh[.] Session adjourned, concluded with prayer.

[end]

Appendix C

STOCKPORT
as noted in the papers, publications, manuscripts, and timelines
of
Clyde Kean Swift
(1909–1993)

(Author's note: Although his family roots were at Swifts, Ohio, below Luke Chute dam, Clyde Kean Swift of Glen Ellyn, Illinois, was born in Stockport in 1909 and, late in life, requested that his ashes be sprinkled on the Muskingum River. His affection for the town, all aspects of the Muskingum River Valley, and especially its steamboat era,[113] generated Clyde's indefatigable Muskingum Valley research, huge volumes of genealogical information, and prolific essays and newspaper series of which the following excerpt is a minute part. My edits are few, mostly trivial, and my clarifications are in brackets.)

> The Muskingum River was the highway for the first settlers of Stockport. They used their canoes to travel to Zanesville and to Marietta as well as visiting neighbors a mile away.

> It was a rare cabin that had a kitchen stove. Cooking was done at the fireplace. No one had a match. A tinder box, with flint and steel, was used. The hunter's gun was fired by a flint, as in the Revolutionary War. The hunter himself had probably been in that war. The settlers' hoe, rake, and plow were of wood. His clothes, homespun. Nothing in the valley moved except by nature, horse, ox, or man. Steam, which was used in a Marietta mill and in steamboats on the Ohio river, had not yet gone up the Muskingum.

---

[113] Clyde said his life-long fascination with the Muskingum stemmed from the stories his father, James Newell Swift [1866-1952], had told him when Clyde was a boy. His father had been a cabin boy on a steamboat on the Muskingum. Clyde wrote, "[James] Newell Swift, nephew of Sam Swift, was cabin boy and steward on the steamboat "Gen'l H. F. Devol" in 1882-84. He lived at Swifts, Oakland, and the Buck farm, as a youth." (Clyde Swift, manuscript, "Beverly-Waterford Steamboat Men," no date.) Clyde's mother was Annie (*nee*) Penrose Swift [1872-1959].

On Jan 9, 1824, the steamboat "Rufus Putnam" set up the river from Marietta; [it] spent the night at Luke Chute, and passed Silverheels Ripple[114] the next morning. If she stopped there it was for wood to fire her boiler. James Leget, Sr., was her pilot on this trip. He was a Waterford man who later lived at Stockport.

The tiny steamboats "Hope" and "Speedwell" came up past Silverheels Ripple in 1827, but most of the settlers' needs were brought by keelboat.[115] At Silverheels an ox team was kept in readiness to help them across the Ripple.

Until 1842 there were few steamboats to bring goods to Silverheels landing, but many keelboats. Each bore a name. They carried such items as: "3 Keggs, 15 bbls Tobacco, 3 pieces linen, 1 bundle of leather, 6 bags of coffee, 1 bale Spanish tobacco, 1 hogshead of liquor, 1 box of cooking tools, 2 bundles of Bedding, 1 portman teau with clothing, 1 tierce of rice, 1 bag cordage." [For example, and of special interest here:]

Keelboat "Friendship," Master Harris White, [left Marietta] for Zanesville April 15, 1834 Marietta to Cazzain Kusle[116], [at] Frisby's Landing [a.k.a. Roxbury, to deliver] 1 bbl Cooking Tools, 1 Cable. 50 cents for Lot & charges 25 cents. To Jeff Sidwell, Silverheels Riffle [Stockport], 2 copper kettles, .50 & $1.25 charges.[117] [then on] To R. Fulton [*et. al.*, at] McConnelsville.[118]

---

[114] Silverheels Riffle (or Ripple) was located at the first bend in the river below the Stockport dam, opposite the mouth of Turkey Run. Now it is usually submerged and subdued by the slackwater created by the dam at Luke Chute. It is named for the Shawnee Silverheels, who lived upstream at the mouth of Bald Eagle Creek, a distance of 0.7 miles [Google Earth]. Silverheels was a brother of Chief Cornstalk (xxxx-1777), Nimwha (xxxx-1780), and their distinguished and oft-cited sister Nonhelema (c. 1718-1786). Late in her life, the U.S. Congress reimbursed Nonhelema for several heads of cattle which U.S. soldiers, *as ordered*, had stolen from her herd in southern Ohio to feed U.S. Army troops garrisoned at forts along the Ohio River during the Indian war. (See Walker, *Where Is the Legendary Silverheels*, 1980, p. 39).
[115] "The first keelboat that navigated the Muskingum River was the Zanesville Rambler, Captain James T. Hahn, owner and master. He [left Zanesville and] arrived in Pittsburgh, June 18, 1823, with a cargo of cotton."
[116] An unknown person or place or a typographical error.
[117] A copy of the original bill of lading of the shipment to Jesse Sidwell at "Silverheels Riffle" (i.e., pre-Stockport) on April 15, 1834, is in Walker, *Stockport, Ohio: A Compendium of Historical Information*, 1984, opposite page 67. Provided courtesy of the late Jerry Devol.
[118] Its next stop was McConnelsville/Malta where those who received goods were R. Fulton, L. D. Barker, Henry Dawes, and J. A. Gilaspie [sic]. The items they received, cost, etc., are omitted here.

After the State appropriated $400,000, March 4, 1836, the engineers embarked at Zanesville on a super flatboat, complete with dining room, kitchen and bunks, to survey the river for dams and locks. A dam was scheduled to be built at Ludlow, in the bend above Hooksburg and a contract awarded to Crossen, Bell, and Taggart. However, the location was changed to Windsor (Silverheels Ripple), after the people in that vicinity subscribed $3,000 to have it relocated. Work on the Windsor Dam started in the spring of 1837 and navigation of the river was obstructed during the six years of work. Boats had to load and unload at the dams, until September 17, 1841, when the steamboat "Tuscarawas" left Zanesville for Marietta. The next day, Saturday the 18th, the Windsor landing was piled high waiting for the "Tuscarawas," the first to pay toll for the trip. She carried freight and passengers to Zanesville or Marietta or in-between.

On Nov. 30th the steamboat "Muskingum" arrived from Pittsburgh at Windsor on her weekly trip to Zanesville. The contractors for the dams and locks invested their profits in land along the river. Arthur Taggart, [who was born in County Tyrone, Ireland] bought 100s of acres on both sides of the Muskingum in the Windsor area.[119] His residence became the present "Silverheels Farm" across from Stockport. In 1842 the first mill was built at Windsor. In that year there were three boats stopping at Stockport twice a week in the Zanesville-Pittsburgh trade and one in the Zanesville-Marietta trade stopping each day.

---

[119] Arthur Taggert became the largest landowner in Morgan County. See the segment of the "Windsor Township Map of Landowners in 1854" on p. 50. "Arthur Taggart, in 1839, bought 600 acres of land near the Stockport Lock for $2,035, including what is known as the 'Silverheels Farm.' In Windsor Twp. up to 1844 he paid $35,000 for land near the river, including several lots in Stockport. The next 11 years he bought $15,444 more land." (Clyde K. Swift, *Muskingum Years 1841,* 1980).

Appendix D

"Keelboats Crews: A Wondrous Race"
by
R. E. Banta[120]

The keelboatmen were tough enough but they were by no means desperadoes. Half the time their work was inconceivably grueling. For keelboats, unlike flats, carried cargo not only downstream, but poled, rowed, and dragged it upstream as well. They grew tough, those keelboatmen, in their terrific exertions and they liked their relaxation to be equally strenuous. The Robin Hoodish aura that surrounds them probably grew because, like many men whose pay comes the hardest, they could be wildly generous upon occasion, and because they usually seem to have confined their more murderous pastimes to the circle of their immediate acquaintanceship or at least to their own social stratum. The fact that occasionally in their roistering they burned, tore down, or pushed into the river whole neighborhoods of river towns was usually overlooked by the law on the grounds that those must have been undesirable sections of the community anyway, since boatmen could have had no reason or desire to visit any other sort.

Every river town had such an undesirable district, but from the very beginning of Ohio River traffic some towns were recognized as being more dissolute, more lawless than others, and—perish the thought!—an unprejudiced visitor may still identify a few of them after two hundred years of progress and culture. To the eyes of keelboatmen no stigma attached to a community so marked, far from it! If a town had a really malodorous repute it was to them, then, an excellent place to lie over and relax a bit. Their relaxing, of course, did nothing to quiet the scene of their repose.

---

[120] Excerpted from R. E. Banta (1904-1977), *The Ohio,* pp. 254-60, (Rinehart & Company, New York, 1949), Chapter Eight, "The Adventurous, The Murderous And The Ring-Tailed Snorters." The title above is not Banta's title, rather his description of keelboatmen which I adopted here. –RW

Contrary to the impression easily gained from a study of the WPA murals in modern [1940s] river-town post offices, the keelboat hand was not necessarily handsome, though he was doubtless of appearance rakishly dashing enough. He usually carried upon his person one or more marks of his avocation; most frequently it was a damaged ear, sometimes bitten off, sometimes cauliflowered . . ., or most often simply chawed in a scalloped design around its rim. Or he could have lost the fleshy portion of his nose and sometimes, if he was unusually inept as a fighter, he could have lost that decorative feature and an ear—or an ear and a half, or even two ears. If, in addition to any or all these misfortunes, he happened to be a veteran of an Indian foray in which he had got himself scalped (it was not at all uncommon to be scalped while unconscious from a wound and to survive the operation), he was likely to present a rather frazzled appearance; one which could not be rendered attractive even by his red-flannel shirt, remaining hair worn in a shoulder-length bob, wool hat set off with a feather, and skin pants—both skin in material and skin tight in cut.

There were some general social distinctions between those who floated or poled the Ohio before steam took over and these methods of propulsion disappeared.

Lowest in the scale were rafters, unloved greenhorns . . . who lashed together any number of logs or timbers from six up, built a lean-to on one end, loaded on their scanty household effects if they were emigrants, or trade goods if commerce was their aim, and floated off downstream. They were practically at the mercy of the current and its many random whims sent them butting and nosing whatever came in the way, from shore line to passing boats.

If the owner was an emigrant he beached his craft when he saw a likely spot—current permitting—and broke it up to use the timber in putting up shelter, if that appeared convenient. Or, if it looked easier to fell new trees, he simply "let her set" to be floated off by the first freshet and later to bring anathema on his anonymous head as it menaced navigation on its way to the Gulf [of Mexico]. Few of these raftin' settlers had much truck with land purchase, titles, or such business; being of a class whom rafting suited, they were perfectly willing to squat upon a likely plot until the owner drove them off or wearied of trying and let them stay.

If bent upon trade, the rafter swapped his "notions" as he went along—and being a *rafter's* notions they were not likely to be what is called class merchandise. He then disposed of what remained, along with the logs of his raft, at New Orleans, and started back east afoot or stopped along the way as the spirit moved him.

Next above the rafter in the social scale came the emigrant flatboatman. He might never have seen navigable water until he embarked on it but his boat made some pretense of answering her helm, and sometimes, if he was affluent and cautious, he hired a pilot. Just above him came the cargo flatboat, which, while built for a one-way trip downstream, was usually commanded by someone who had made the trip before.

The bulk of emigration westward on the river by more substantial people was by flatboat. Building of such craft at Pittsburgh or Wheeling, or wherever a good road from the settlements struck the upper river, became an important industry. Flatboats could be built to survive almost any amount of banging which even the island-studded Ohio could give them, or they could be thrown together of a combination of green and rotten planks and shoddy workmanship so that they were scarcely able to float their own weight in a moderate riffle. Emigrants were warned against purchasing the latter article by newspapers, land agents, emigrants' guidebooks, and well-disposed rivermen. But through impatient haste, ignorance, bullheadedness, or the persuasive lies of the builders they often did so anyway. The result was sometimes that the members of an emigrant family were marooned by the river scores of miles from a settlement without gun, ax, or means of making fire and with only what woodcraft they had picked up in the cities of New York, Philadelphia, Baltimore, or even (perish the thought!) Boston.

Cargo flatboats were something else again. They were usually built by, or to the order of, the jobber of produce or the association of the farmers who supplied the cargo. No chances were taken in their construction (except by some occasional obstinate cuss who wouldn't ask or accept advice) and the wood employed was carefully selected in order to be salable at New Orleans.

These cargo boats were built wherever the products to be supplied originated. The Monongahela and later the Kentucky River produced whisky and most tributaries that ran through beech or oak tree land in Ohio, Indiana, and Kentucky contributed hogs fattened on "mast," which were shipped in the form of hams and pickled sides and shoulders of pork. The Kentucky River farmers loaded hemp and tobacco, those on the Wabash offered shelled corn, cherry and walnut plants, ginseng, and so on.

The flatboats carrying produce were usually manned by the owners, their neighbors, and their sons, who, once cargo and boat were sold at New Orleans, walked or rode horseback up the Natchez Trace to Kentucky and the Midwest or took passage on upstream keelboats and later steamboats, if the value of their cargo had been great enough to warrant such extravagance.

If owner and crew succeeded in eluding the bandits who lined the Trace, the social charms of New Orleans, Natchez-under-the-Hill, Memphis, Shawneetown, and other riverside communities which featured gilded sin as a local commodity, and got home with their money, they could and frequently did pay for great tracts of rich river-bottom land with the proceeds of a few such trips. . . .

But high in the scale above even the most experienced flatboaters stood the before-mentioned keelboatmen—at least until they were supplanted in the esteem of the marveling public by the guady and princely rich steamboat pilots of the forties and fifties, complete with the doeskin vest and tremendous watch chains that were the badge of office.

The keelboaters were the aristocracy of the early day; their gaudy life the preference of every ten-year-old boy, and the secret envy, often, of his grandfather.

This upper crust of rivermen was composed, by its own admission, of genuine ring-tailed snorters from away back; children of calamity and bearers of ill tidings who could lick their weight in catamounts with their bare teeth while handcuffed, who could outdrink, outfight, and outcuss anything in this world or the next. The reason for this necessary supremacy in matters of strength and stamina? Why, solely that *they* poled, rowed, or snaked their boats *up*stream as well as steered them down! *They* were the official cargo carriers, the preservers of upriver commerce—until, or course, an even more fiery monster, the steamboat, took over.

They were tough—there was no question about that—and though they were not wantonly murderous . . . they were boisterous and reckless. . . . They were loud in the announcement of their iniquity to every shore dweller, every raftman, every flatboater they sighted. . . .

The keelers were feared ashore (although their free-spent money was always welcome) because they were possessed of a strong fraternal spirit which prompted them, when one of their number had been inordinately mulcted in either a gambling establishment or a house of dubious repute to (*a*) push the building into the river if it happened to be located at the river's edge, as many were, or (*b*) if that was impractical either to pull it board from board or to set fire to it.

The shore dwellers were not viewed as mortal enemies by the keelers, however, nor were even the rafters whose erratic progress presented such real danger to their lives. As is usual it was the next below themselves in the social scale, the flatboatmen, for whom their special venom was reserved. By report the battles between these two classes, sometimes held upon keelboats hooked to flatboats midstream, sometimes in riverside towns, sometimes on islands selected for the purpose by challenge and acceptance, were fearful to behold.

Tough and practiced in the manly art of self-defense as they were, the keelers often fought on only even terms with Hoosier, Red-hoss Kaintuck, Buckeye, and Sucker farm boys who, though uninformed in the finer points of the art of mayhem, had still been somewhat hardened by stump pullin', loggin', and, as was claimed by many of them, "pushin' a plow and two ox too" through prairie sod or bottom land choked with pea vines and bear grass.

Those were colorful days on the Ohio and its tributaries and on the Mississippi; considerably more attractive in the usual retelling, probably, than they were in actual fact. Perhaps it was as well that, by 1830 or so, the keelers were obviously going—to reappear later as bodacious loggers—the rafts were thinning out and the worst menaces to peaceful travel on the Ohio had become card sharks and steamboat-boiler explosions.

Appendix E

Who Was Caleb Swan, Jr.?

Original 2005/Revised 2024

In November, 2002, newspaper correspondent Craig Linder filed an article from Washington, D.C., "Memorials Recognize U.S. Sacrifice." He wrote:

> With its rich military history Washington offers visitors dozens of attractions related to the U.S. armed forces. These five sites are among the best-known tributes to the nation's service men and women: The Iwo Jima Memorial, Women's Memorial, African-American Civil War Memorial, Korean War Veterans Memorial, and the Arlington National Cemetery." Regarding the latter he noted, "More than 260,000 people are buried here, among them men as prominent as President John F. Kennedy and as anonymous as Revolutionary War veteran Caleb Swan.[1]

Anonymous? Caleb Swan, Jr., son of Caleb Swan, Sr. (1718-1793) and Dorothy *nee* Frye (1731-1821), was born on July 2, 1758, in Methuen, Essex County, Massachusetts.[2] During the Revolutionary War in 1776, he served as sergeant of artificers[3]; on February 1, 1777, he became a corporal in the 9th Massachusetts; on November 26, 1779, he was appointed ensign. On January 1, 1781, he was transferred to the 8th Massachusetts Continental infantry; that year he was Captain of the Essex County militia under Colonel Samuel Johnson. On June 12, 1783, he transferred to the 3rd Massachusetts and was retained in Jackson's Continental Regiment until November, 1783. He served in the military until June 20, 1784.[4]

On November 2, 1783, while Swan was still in uniform, General Washington bade his troops farewell, the army began to disband, and each soldier sought his separate fortune. In the five years that followed, under the Articles of Confederation, the central government was virtually non-existent and what did exist was broke and/or broken. An intermittent Congress, under the Confederation, often doubled as a court and had virtually no executive branch. Executive decisions were left to boards, such as the Committee of States, that seldom met and, when they did meet, they often lacked a quorum thus could not do business.

A major crisis faced by the new Confederation Congress was nothing less than an armed mutiny of soldiers from Pennsylvania who, on June 21, 1783, with bayonets fixed, marched to the statehouse in Philadelphia where Congress was in session. With sentinels placed at every door, the mutineers threatened to "let loose an enraged soldiery" on the delegates if their demands were not met "within 20 minutes." Their grievance was lack of pay. A few days later, Congress temporarily moved from Philadelphia to Trenton, New Jersey.

To many Americans at that time, the idea of a standing army was considered a dangerous idea. But to many others, the attempted mutiny in Philadelphia proved the need. In either case, it was clear that government required a centrally-controlled military force to combat hostile Indians on its frontiers, restrain squatters from violating Indian treaties, protect surveyors, and maintain peace between squabbling territories and/or states. State militia were too diverse, dispersed, undisciplined, parochial, and not under federal control.

Particularly on the frontier, militia vigilantes often made things worse, not better. Their cruel and wanton acts inflamed tribes, causing them to retaliate against innocent settlers, form alliances, and agitate for general war. For example, the blackest day in Ohio history was the work of state militia. On March 8, 1782, under Col. David Williamson, militiamen from Washington County, Pennsylvania, murdered 96 unarmed Christian Indians gathering their corn at Gnadenhutten on the upper Muskingum. At councils and treaties spanning decades, chief after chief recited long lists of such abuses and injustices they had suffered at the hands of borderers, militia, and arrogant, dictatorial, U.S. army officers sent by Washington to serve as treaty "negotiators."

On March 8, 1785, the Confederation Congress elected General Henry Knox as Secretary of War. He accepted on the 17th. On April 1, Congress resolved that 700 troops were necessary to protect its western lands which the states and tribes had ceded to the federal government. The immediate task was to evict squatters from the territory north of the Ohio River, protect both private and public surveyors, and escort treaty negotiators. But authorizing troops for the western frontier was easier than recruiting them.

Daniel Shay's Rebellion in Massachusetts in September, 1786, revealed the inadequacy of the army and the impotence of the central government. Congress was stunned by the uprising. In response, a month later Congress dramatically increased the number of non-commissioned officers and privates to 2,040.[5]

Swan was one of few officers who continued in federal service under the Articles of Confederation and beyond.[6] The entire "Pentagon" in 1786, in addition to Secretary of War Henry Knox, consisted of three clerks and a messenger.[7] The three clerks in 1787 were chief clerk William Knox (the boss's brother), John Staff, Jr., and Caleb Swan, Jr., age 29. Each clerk, as set by Congress, was paid $450 a year.[8] Occasionally, they hired a laborer to chop firewood, etc.

On occasion, Secretary Knox sent Swan to the western or southern frontier, entrusting him with money or warrants to pay troops, contractors, and salaries of government officials.[9] Soon Swan's rank and importance increased. During the early 1790s, promoted to Lieutenant, Swan served as U.S. ambassador to the Creek Indians in Alabama.[10] Historians of Native Americans in that region yet cite Swan's notes. For example, a recent work on Creek leaders, in discussing the racial admixtures to the tribe, noted that

"…army lieutenant and deputy Indian agent Swan set the white population among the Creeks in 1790 at three hundred," a number, Swan added, "sufficient to contaminate all the natives."[11]

In 1791, Swan was again among the Coushatta and Creek Indians in Alabama. He wrote, "…old Red-Shoe, king of the Alabamas and Coosades [Coushatta]" was one of the five "most influential chiefs of the country either in peace or in war."[12] In one candid entry, Swan noted that one Creek woman was "thick-necked, ugly, and extremely masculine." Swan's work, from which the above quotes are taken, is, "Position and State of Manners and Arts in the Creek, or Muscogee Nation in 1791."[13] Dependable deputy Indian agent Swan would soon land a better job.

Paymaster of the U.S. Army

The change from a Continental Congress, to a Confederation Congress, to a Constitutional Congress abolished and replaced every aspect of civil governance except one — the military. The Continental Congress created a Board of War and Ordnance on June 12, 1776, then replaced it with a War Department, to be headed by a Secretary at War, on February 7, 1781. On October 30, Major General Benjamin Lincoln was named the first Secretary at War. The War Department was the only department of the central government that continued unchanged under the three governments. It included the Office of Paymaster.[14]

As the mutiny in the "Pennsylvania line" suggested, an army can survive without a lot of things, but a paymaster is not one of them. As early as June 16, 1775 — a year before it created the Board of War and Ordnance — the Continental Congress created a Pay Department for the army. The Department comprised the Paymaster-General and one Deputy, at $100 and $50 per month, respectively. On July 27, 1775, Congress elected James Warren of Massachusetts to the post. After Warren resigned, Congress, on April 27, 1776, elected Washington's aide-de-camp, William Palfrey of Massachusetts, to the post. Palfrey served ably during the Revolution but, in late 1780, on a trip to France to purchase military supplies, his ship was lost at sea and all aboard perished.[15]

On January 17, 1781, Congress elected John Pierce of Connecticut, the Commissioner of Army Accounts, to replace Palfrey. Pierce took on both duties. After six years, on March 23, 1787, Congress officially combined both jobs under one title, the Commissioner of Army Accounts. Unfortunately, in August, 1788, Pierce died. Joseph Howell, Jr., was selected Commissioner of Army Accounts, which continued to include all paymaster duties.[16]

The first Constitutional Congress held its initial session on March 4, 1789, in New York City and, the next month, declared George Washington as president. Despite a huge influx of resumes from Revolutionary War veterans seeking appointments in the new government, Congress, in September, decided to continue Henry Knox as Secretary of War. In turn, with only minor changes, Knox kept his staff, Swan included, and later added a few new ones. They all received a pay raise. By law, Knox received $3000 a year; Swan and the others, " not more than $500."

President Washington and Secretary of War Knox soon received terrible news. On October 19-22, 1790, in western Ohio, the Indian confederation defeated General Josiah Harmar's army. Although Harmar's stinging defeat was a setback for the ambitions of the nascent government, the worst was yet to come. Late the next year, on November 4, 1791, near the future Indiana border north of Cincinnati, the Indian confederation slaughtered General Arthur St. Clair's U.S. Army. Worse than Harmar's defeat, losses were staggering. When news of the prodigious slaughter of the army reached Philadelphia, President Washington was livid, called St. Clair "worse than a murderer," and demanded his resignation from the military.[17]

On the one hand, generals in the field cited the poor administration of the War Department as a major cause of the disasters; on the other, authorities in Philadelphia cited poor army discipline and bad judgment by commanders in the field ("tactical blunders") as the primary cause. Whereas Washington blamed St. Clair's mismanagement, St. Clair blamed the government's delayed shipments, shoddy supplies, lack of boats, and shortage of horses. Both were true. And all sides, of course, blamed the army contractors for delays and shoddy materiel. In one instance, for example, all the guns shipped to St. Clair's army were defective. St. Clair himself was not well, taking various pain medications, and could not get on or off a horse by himself.

But other issues nobody wanted to face. The young, energetic General Josiah Harmar, after whom the frontier fort built in 1785 at the mouth of the Muskingum River had been named, was an alcoholic. In one joint operation, Harmar was so drunk and confused as to the chain of military command that he obeyed orders issued by the Governor of Virginia rather than the Secretary of War.[18] Knox was not amused! General James Wilkinson in Kentucky complained that Harmar "…was not only addicted to drink, but was also a bad disciplinarian."[19] Knox, however, refused to recognize or do anything about it. President Washington, when learning the details of Harmar's military defeat, remarked to Knox, "I expected little from it from the moment I heard he was a drunkard."[20] Among the charges against him during the inquiry into the causes of his defeat, Harmer was accused of being drunk on duty. Although acquitted of the charge, Harmar resigned from the military on January 1, 1792, and went home to Pennsylvania.

Another issue was the army itself. Frontiersmen, recruited for brief tours of duty, were neither prepared nor motivated to fight, thus generally made poor soldiers. Most recruits joined simply to get a good set of clothes.[21] Discipline was so difficult to maintain that floggings and lashings were virtually daily occurrences at Fort Harmar and other military outposts on the frontier. What should one expect, wondered Cincinnati land tycoon John Cleves Symmes, from troops made up of men "…purchased from prisons, wheelbarrows and brothels at $2 per month."[22] Knox's friend, Revolutionary War veteran Henry Jackson, had warned Knox at the outset that, given the army pay scale, the army should expect nothing but "Vagabonds… and the very dregs of other nations."[23]

On St. Clair's campaign against the Indians, wives, girlfriends, and prostitutes traveled through the wilderness with the army. Given the on-going official inquiry into Harmar's drinking, St. Clair, in poor health, taking a host of medications, and wrapped in blankets, with his army already on the march, decided to restrict drinking among the troops. Morale plummeted, especially among the free-spirited and the spirits-loving militiamen from Kentucky. Morale was so low and desertions so high that, on one occasion, St. Clair had several deserters caught and hanged before the troops during a routine military parade. In reaction, several days later 60 more men deserted![24]

St. Clair was made to appear before official courts of inquiry into the fiasco. But, in the end, the government held no one accountable. Although Washington forced St. Clair to resign his military commission, St. Clair continued his appointment as Governor of the Northwest Territory. Congress responded by doing what bureaucracies always do—reorganize the Department. As if to complete the farce, in early 1792 Knox dispatched Swan to Kentucky to pay the truculent Kentucky militiamen for their so called "service" under St. Clair.

As part of its reorganization, on May 8, 1792, the Constitutional Congress reestablished the Office of Paymaster as a separate office. The paymaster, as before, had "to reside near the headquarters of the troops of the United States" and his duties were "to receive, from the treasurer, all the moneys which shall be entrusted to him for the purpose of paying the pay, the arrears of pay, subsistence or forage, due to the troops of the United States." Then, after examining and certifying the pay accounts, he was to issue warrants for payment.[25] Congress trusted Washington; Washington trusted Knox; and Knox trusted Swan. That same day, as a part of the reorganization, President Washington named Caleb Swan to the post, Paymaster of the Army of the United States.

Washington did not want peace, but Ohio. Thus there was urgent work to be done—conquering the Indians, seizing Ohio, and using it to grant land bounties which the Revolutionary Government had promised its officers, soldiers, and sailors. Next, the task of recruiting, drilling, fielding, and commanding an effective army fell to General Anthony Wayne. And he did. The methodical, cautious, sober Wayne defeated the Indian forces near the mouth of the Maumee River on August 20, 1794.

Whether Swan was with Wayne's expedition down the Maumee or waited at Cincinnati is unclear. Cincinnati newspapers occasionally mentioned him and the local post office at the end of 1794 indicated that Swan had an unclaimed letter. Years later, Swan wrote that he had entered "…the Army, raised for the defense of the Frontiers against the native savages under General Anthony Wayne, on the 8th of May 1792…and served on the said frontiers upwards of seven years, in the capacity of Pay Master of the Army of the United States."[26]

In summer, 1795, Swan attended the grand treaty negotations at Greeneville between the United States and the Wyandot, Delaware, Shawnee, Ottawa, Chippewa, Pottawatomie, Miami, Eel River, Kickapoo, and Kaskaskia. On August 3, 1795, in his official capacity as army paymaster, Swan, along with 90 Indian leaders and chiefs, including Miami Chief Little Turtle, various U.S. officials (e.g., William Henry Harrison), and 20 or so interpreters and assistants (e.g., former Indian captive-gone-native, Isaac Zane, son of Ebenezer Zane of Wheeling, served as one of the translators) signed the treaty. In his will, one of the three friends whom Swan asked to take care of his children was Francis Scott Key.

The Ohio Company at Marietta

In the aftermath of Wayne's victory, both Ohio Company stockholders and settlers, frustrated by more than four years of frontier warfare, were eager to claim, if not occupy, the land. In late 1794 and throughout 1795, in anticipation of a favorable treaty, Ohio Company surveyors from Marietta marked off the remaining borders and lots in the Ohio Company Purchase. On February 1, 1796, just four months after the treaty officially extinguished the Indians' claims to southern Ohio, Ohio Company stockholders—representing 819 of the original 1,000 shares—met at Marietta to disperse its final land assets. As noted, each company share was worth 1,173 acres as follows: one 3-, 8-, 100- 160-, 262-, and 640-acre lot (= 1,173), plus a one-third acre city lot.[27]

Swan, who never lived in the Muskingum Valley, owned one share, thus was entitled to 1,173 acres.[28] When, how, and and why he first obtained his share is not known. Of his six lots of different acreages, Swan's 100-acre lot, presumably based on the luck of the draw, was Lot #90 in Range XI, Township IX. This lot was a long, narrow, east-west rectangle spanning the Muskingum, half on one side, half on the other, in the northernmost part of the Ohio Company Purchase. The lot comprised rich, level bottoms on each side of the river, stretching back to wooded hilltops beyond—specifically, pre-Stockport. Lot #90 is that part of the village that lies on the north side of Broadway Street (SR-266) and extends east across the Muskingum (beyond the late John Porter farm). Main Street runs through the center of the western half of Lot#90 lengthwise.[29]

It is not known whether Swan ever saw his land. Virtually all of the first landowners in the Stockport area were shareholders in the Ohio Company. Many invested in the Ohio Company, not to develop the land, but to speculate in western real estate. Indicative, consider the original owners of the lots near Swan's Lot #90. Among prominent figures in the military, the Ohio Company, and the U.S. government were:

General Josiah Harmar (Lot #94); Territorial Governor and General Arthur St. Clair, former President of the Confederation Congress in 1787 (Lot #92); Territorial Judge Winthrop Sargent (Lot #78); author of the Ordinance of 1787, Rev. Manasseh Cutler of Ipswich, Massachusetts, who negotiated the Ohio Company contract with Congress in 1787 (Lot #1062); attorney William R. Putnam, son of General Rufus Putnam, Superintendent of the Ohio Company (Lots #1054 and #1055); medical doctor and future Marietta historian Samuel P. Hildreth of Methuen, Massachusetts (Lot #1042); former Indian trader (1772), Indian agent (1774), Army Quartermaster at Fort Pitt, and Pittsburgh businessman, James O'Hara (Lot #88); Justice of the Peace, Judge of the Court of Common Pleas, Judge of the Probate Court, and later Territorial Judge, Joseph Gilman (Lot #77); Clerk of the Court of Common Pleas, Benjamin Ives Gilman (Lot #69); and not least, Melancthon Smith, a member of the Confederation Congress in New York who had approved the Ordinance of 1787 (Lot #1037), and the Postmaster General of the United States and Treasurer of the U.S. Congress Ebenezer Hazard (Lot #1060) — all within a few miles of pre-Stockport (Lot #90).[30] When the Ohio Company dispersed its land assets in 1796, of its 817 shareholders *less than a third had ever lived in Ohio.* Two notable examples: Thomas Jefferson owned a city lot in Marietta, now a city park which slopes down to the Muskingum, and Revolutionary War ship commander John Paul Jones was granted two entire townships—Rome and Canaan—now in Athens County, Ohio.

In late 1795 or early 1796 in Cincinnati, perhaps enroute back from the Treaty of Greeneville, Swan sold his Muskingum Lot #90 to Major Thomas Doyle of Cincinnati, price unknown.[31] This was likely Thomas Doyle, III (1759/c1800), who had been badly wounded in St. Clair's disastrous Indian defeat in November, 1791, and the man whom General Anthony Wayne had sent in 1794 to rebuild the old French-era fort at Fort Massac on the Ohio River at present-day Metropolis, Illinois.

On June 26, 1796, Doyle then sold Lot #90 to Charles Vattier and his wife Pamela of Cincinnati for $200. This was an indenture pending until "…regular deeds are issued by the Muskingum Company."[32] About the same time, the colorful Vattier petitioned Congress for land in the French Grant, a small parcel of land on the Ohio River which Congress granted to Frenchmen whom the defunct Scioto Land Company, years before, had defrauded. Ironically in 1807 Vattier himself was convicted of burglary and larceny, i.e., "stealing from the Office of the Receiver of Public Notes for the District of Cincinnati large sums in Specie and Bank Notes." Exhibits at his trial included "many curious traits in the culprit's life . . . ."[33] What traits were not stated.

In all, Lot #90 sold four times in Cincinnati before a settler purchased the land. The last Cincinnati owner, Nicolas Longworth, held it for more than nine years! Not until Frederick Eveland, its sixth owner, purchased Lot #90 in October, 1816, did the lot become locally owned.[34] Thus, it was twenty years after the Ohio Company stockholders' meeting divided the land in 1796, before Lot #90 ceased being an object of real estate speculation and was occupied by an owner. As the list and time lapses cited suggest, in the Ohio Company on the Muskingum, landsharks and elites got rich, while "the poorer sort," as

Rufus Putnam called westward migrants and poor war veterans, got axes, blisters, venereal diseases, and/or tomahawked.[35]

After the Treaty of Greeneville, Swan's duties took him to Michigan territory. In 1796, 60-year-old Rev. David Jones, Baptist missionary who had toured Indian villages in Ohio in 1772 and 1773 to preach the gospel and who, 24 years later, attended and signed the Treaty of Greeneville as Chaplain of the U.S. Army, was stationed at Detroit. Jones noted in his journal November 2, 1796, "Settled with Caleb Swan, P.M.G., to the last day of October, 1796, forage rations and pay. He paid me two hundred and thirty dollars."[36]

The next year at Detroit, beginning in August, Swan kept a journal of his month-long trip on Lakes Sinclair, Michigan, and Superior, noting the topography, weather, temperature, and, of course, the Indians.[37] In 1798, based on his observations and experiences, Swan wrote an article, "Some Account of the Northwestern Lakes of America."[38] He continued on the frontier until July, 1799, when he was called back to the capital at Philadelphia. In June, 1800, by order of President John Adams, the capital moved to Washington City, where Swan continued as Army Paymaster, married[39], had a daughter[40], and lived the rest of his life.

Caleb Swan Jr.'s 100-acre lot at pre-Stockport was incidental to his wealth. As early as 1801 he owned a major part of a 4,000-acre tract, pooled from soldiers' land warrants, located just east of Coshocton.[41] This land lay in the U.S. Military District, a region between Zanesville and Millersburg set aside by the government in 1796 to be given to Revolutionary War soldiers in parcels based on rank (See page 15). These land bounties were of little or no use to the vast majority of war veterans, thus they were forced to sell their titles to land jobbers for a pittance or get nothing. Many, if not most, were sold in New York City to speculators and agents who, by law, were forced to aggregate them into large pools of thousands of acres before anyone could legally settle on the land.[42]

As well, by 1808, Swan, in addition to his home in Washington City, owned three improved farms about eight miles north of Cincinnati, a square in the city of Cincinnati, 77.5 acres "on the Big Hill" 16 miles from Cincinnati, and another 1,700 acres near Zanesville. In addition to his house and property in Washington, he owned three slaves — Susan and her two daughters "Airy" (Ariande), and Caroline — whom he willed to his wife.[43]

Country Cousins at Waterford, Ohio

Caleb Swan, Jr., had more than a professional and financial interest in the Muskingum Valley. Lieutenant Joseph Frye (1765-1814) of Waterford, Ohio, was born May 19, 1765, in the same town in Massachusetts as Caleb Swan. (Local legend claims that Frye, about age eight, had served as a drummer boy at the Battle of Bunker Hill.)

Frye, at age 24, emigrated to Marietta, Ohio, in 1789. He soon joined the settlers at Waterford and was living there when northern Indians surprised and killed twelve Ohio

Company settlers at Big Bottom (one mile down the Muskingum River from pre-Stockport Lot 90) on January 2, 1791, then fled up the Sandusky-Muskingum trail with four white male captives. (One died in captivity; two worked their way back to their homes in New England; and one returned to the Muskingum and died at Belpre, Ohio.) After the massacre, Frye urged the terrified settlers at Waterford to build a fort on the east bank of the Muskingum. He designed the odd, three-sided fort and the settlers and soldiers, after an Indian attack on the fort was successfully repelled, honored him by giving the fort his name. It stood near the river behind present-day (2024) Fort Frye High School.

Methuen and Andover, Massachusetts, a few miles apart, were home to Swan and Frye families for generations. Caleb Swan, Jr.'s, mother was Dorothy *nee* Frye of Andover. Joseph Frye, born in 1765, and Swan, born in 1758, were second cousins. Indicative, Caleb Swan, Jr. had a younger brother born in 1761 named Joseph Frye Swan.

The Frye family boasts a long military tradition, dating back to the French and Indian War. In addition to his mother's maiden name, it is not surprising that Swan, Jr., in his will gave his city block in Cincinnati, as well as 77.5 acres outside of the city, to "Nathaniel Frye, junr my nephew." As noted, Caleb Swan, Jr., and Lieut. Joseph Frye, for whom Fort Frye at Beverly, Ohio, was named, were second cousins.[44][45] (See p. 13.)

By virtue of his service in the Revolution, his extensive travels to southern, western, and northern frontiers, his government job headquartered in the nation's capitals at Philadelphia and Washington, and his work among various Indian tribes, Swan was well known across a vast space and time. His name is sprinkled in records from Alabama to Detroit, from Cincinnati to New York. His name is found in the correspondence or records of prominent Americans such as George Washington, Alexander Hamilton, Meriwether Lewis, and William Henry Harrison.[46] He is cited in President Theodore Roosevelt's *The Winning of the West*.[47] As well, Swan authored ethnographic papers that scholars and historians on native Americans have cited.

On June 30, 1808, at age 50, Swan resigned as Paymaster-General of the United States. He died on November 29, 1809, cause unknown, and was buried in the Old Presbyterian Cemetery in Washington, D.C.

Swan was gone but not forgotten. In a ceremony 83 years later on May 12, 1892, Swan's remains, along with the remains of two other Revolutionary War veterans —William W. Burrows and General James House—were removed to Arlington National Cemetery.[48] As shown on the Internet, a stone slab now covers Swan's grave.[49]

As fate would have it, the first white owner of the site of which would become Stockport, Ohio, was a Revolutionary War veteran, clerk in the office of the Secretary of War, Indian agent to the Creek Nation, Paymaster of the U.S. Army, an appointee of President

Washington, signatory of the Treaty of Greeneville, slave owner, author, and owner of thousands of acres in Ohio, and a house in Washington City.

Caleb Swan, Jr., is also one of only ten Revolutionary War soldiers buried at Arlington National Cemetery.[49]

Endnotes to Appendix E

[1] *Detroit Free Press*, November 3, 2002.

[2] Swan states in his initial will, March 24, 1807, that he was born "about 1760." One of the executors of his will was Philip Barton Key, an attorney. Swan stipulated that if his attorney died, the executorship would devolve to Key's nephew, a young attorney living in Georgetown, Francis Scott Key, whose fame came later as a result of the War of 1812. Appreciation is expressed to D. B. Gaddes for summarizing Swan's estate papers in December, 1956. Swan's will and estate papers are housed at the University of Baltimore Library, 1420 Maryland Ave., Baltimore, Maryland 21201.

[3] Swan, Jr., says in his will that "on the 6th of January 1777, entered into the Army of the [now United States] in defense of the then so call'd liberties of this country and was spared to see the end of the war...."

[4] Francis B. Heitman, H*istorical Register of Officers of the Continental Army during the War of the Revolution*, (1914) 1967; The New England Historical and Genealogical Register, Prokasy Library, The New England Historic Genealogical Society, Boston, Massachusetts, pp. 33-45.

[5] Col. A. B. Carey, "The Pay Department," U.S. Army, n.d., p. 3.

[6] Harry M. Ward, *The Department of War*, 1781-1795, 1962, p. 100.

[7] Ward, *op. cit.*, p. 83.

[8] Ward, *op. cit.*, p. 210.

[9] Ward, *op. cit.*, p. 145.

[10] Ward, *op. cit.*, p. 219.

[11] Benjamin W. Griffith, McIntosh and Weatherford: Creek Indian Leaders, 1988, Chapter One.

[12] Quoted in Jim Bradshaw, "Coushatta Heritage Reaches Deep into the Past," Lafayette, Louisiana, *Daily Advertiser*, October 28, 1997.

[13] Henry R. Schoolcraft, *Information Respecting the History, Condition and Prospects of the Indian Tribes of the United States*, Vol. 5, 1855, pp. 251-83.

[14] Ward, *op. cit.*, pp. 2, 7, and 11.

[15] Carey, *op. cit.*, pp. 1-2.

[16] Carey, *op. cit.*, pp. 2-3.

[17] President George Washington: "It's all over. St. Clair's defeated — routed, the officers nearly all killed. ... Here, yes, here on this very spot I took leave of him. ... You have your instructions, I said, from the Secretary of War. I will add but one word — beware of a surprise! You know how the Indians fight us. ... He went off with that as my last solemn warning ... and yet!! to suffer that army to be cut to pieces, hacked, butchered, tomahawked by a surprise — the very thing I guarded him against!! Oh God, Oh God, he is worse than a murderer! How can he answer to his country? The blood of the slain is upon him — the curse of widows and orphans — the curse of Heaven! ... This must not go beyond this room." Wiley Sword, *President Washington's Indian War: The Struggle for the Old Northwest, 1790–1795*, 1985, p. 201.

[18] Ward, *op. cit.*, p. 67.

[19] Theodore Roosevelt, *The Winning of the West*, 1905, Vol. 4, Part 5.

[20] Allan W. Eckert, *A Sorrow in Our Heart: The Life of Tecumseh*, 1992, p. 734.

[21] Ward, *op. cit.*, p. 89.

[22] Ward, *op. cit.*, p. 133.

[23] Ward, *op. cit.*, p. 104.

[24] Ward, op. *cit.*, p. 135.

[25] Ward, *op. cit.*, p. 145.

[26] Swan's *Will*, March 24, 1807.

[27] H. Z. Williams, *History of Washington County*, Ohio, 1881, pp. 92 and 94.

[28] Williams, *op. cit.*, p. 92. Much of the remaining acreage due Swan was granted in the Military District near Zanesville. He held large parcels there until his death. (Will)

[29] Judy Pannier, Ohio Company map, Marietta College, Marietta, Ohio; 1859 Plat Map, Courthouse, McConnelsville, Ohio.

[30] Richard Walker, *Stockport, Ohio*, 1984, Ohio Company Maps, pp. 57-9; See Williams, *op. cit.*

[31] Research by Rebecca Faires, Morgan County Recorder, McConnelsville, Ohio.
[32] Faires, *op. cit.*, p. 33.
[33] Morgan, *Bibliography of Ohio Imprints*, 1796-1850.
[34] Faires, *op. cit.*, p. 35.
[35] Richard Walker, *Wolf Creek and the Muskingum*, 1996.
[36] "Journal of the Rev. David Jones, A.M., Chaplain of the United States Legion," Clarke Historical Library, Central Michigan University, Mount Pleasant, Michigan.
[37] "The Northwest Country in 1797," *Magazine of American History*, Vol. XIX, January, 1888, pp. 774-77.
[38] Appleton's *Cyclopaedia of American Biography*, Vol. 6, 1889, pp. 3-4. See note #48 below.
[39] On August 18, 1806, age 48, Swan married Maria Henreitta Abert, a woman much younger than him, the daughter of John Abert of Shepherdstown, Virginia.
[40] Caleb Swan, Jr.'s, only child was Maria Margaretta Swan. Twenty-two years after Swan died, she wed Captain George Allan Magruder, later a Commodore. He died in Paris on October 17, 1871, and was buried there. She died, age 65, on March 4, 1875, and was buried in Brompton Cemetery, London, England. On November 7, 1876, his body was exhumed and interred in London in the same cemetery as hers. They had at least one daughter, Helen Lady Abinger, who had at least one daughter, Evelina Haberfield.
[41] In early 1801, Swan had his attorney/surveyor in Zanesville, John Matthews, divide this land up for himself (1,550 acres), Richard Allison (1,150 acres), Mahlon Ford (1,100 acres), and Edward Miller (200 acres). In 1804 they respectively had received 1,496, 1,040, 1,033, and 188 acres. (Correspondence, July 14, 1804, Legacy Library, Marietta College, Marietta, Ohio. See also note #43.)
[42] Jim Petro, *Ohio Land: A Short History*, Office of the Auditor of State, 1997, pp. 28-9.
[43] Swan's attorney/surveyor in Zanesville who looked after his interests was John Mathews. Their correspondence is in Special Collections at Legacy Library at Marietta College, Marietta, Ohio.
Range 5, Township 5, Quarter no. 2 in the Military District. (Correspondence, February 13, 1801, Legacy Library, Marietta College. See also note 41.)
[44] Elizabeth Thorniley Owen, *Fort Frye on the Muskingum*, 1932. For a Morgan County account of the death of Lieut. Joseph Frye, "a Waterford settlement school teacher of homely appearance and charming personality," see Reverend Charles Sparrow Nickerson's essay, "Traditions of Muskingum Valley Pioneer Days," in the *McConnelsville Herald*, Vol. 5, p. 1 ff., April 14, 1938. Nickerson (1860–1942), a native of Center Township, Morgan County, Ohio, states that, according to "local tradition," Frye was ambushed, shot, and killed by Indians near Blockhouse Run at Waterford at the close of the War of 1812. Although this account is still (2023) unconfirmed, it also is uncontested. It is puzzling, indeed, that *no other record or account of Frye's death has ever been found*. Nickerson (1938): "We do not know the exact conditions and circumstances that led to the death of Lieutenant Frye. But we do know that all through the war [of 1812] bodies of hostile Indians, in the pay of the enemy [the British via Detroit and Canada] roamed all over Ohio and committed all kinds of depredations. The local tradition is that Lieut. Frye and another man, generally supposed to be his aged relative, Major Asa Coburn, were shot down from ambush upon either side of a small brook called "Blockhouse Run" because it flowed by Fort Tyler, the blockhouse of which was still standing, and that they were buried near where they fell. Their tombstones, with a few others of Revolutionary veterans, were standing as late as 1875, but have since disappeared." (Appreciation is due the late Opal Cooper of Stockport, Ohio, and late Louise Zimmer of Marietta, Ohio, for this information, both of whom were tireless truth-seekers and forthright in all they wrote or said.)
[45] Owen, *op. cit.*, p. 16.
[46] Washington's Papers, Vol. 10, p. 366; *American Exploration: Lewis and Clark*, R. M. Smythe auction document, New York, New York; Audrey Walker, ed., "Alexander Hamilton: A Register of His Papers in the Library of Congress," Washington, D.C., 1997; "William Henry Harrison Papers and Documents, 1791-1864," Indiana Historical Society, Indianapolis, Indiana, 2004.
[47] Roosevelt, *op. cit.*, Vol. 4, Part 5. Appleton's, *op. cit.*, p. 49. See note #38 above.
[48] Swan's grave is located in Arlington National Cemetery in Section 1-301 C.
[49] http://www.arlingtoncemetery.net/calebswa.htm

Appendix F

Endubonah

Approximately a hundred years after the Muskingum River dams and locks were constructed, that is, from the mid-1920s to early 1940s, the plateau areas opposite Luke Chute dam and locks were locally known as The Boy Scout Farm. It was organized under the aegis of the Southeastern Ohio Boy Scout Council.

Marietta businessman Orton C. Dunn (c. 1785—8/30/1933) was its moving spirit. He had enjoyed the site as a lad, thus, as an adult, during and after his successful career in the oil and gas business both in Oklahoma and in the Muskingum Valley, he bought the land for a boy scout reservation.

He named it Endubonah, an Indian word which means "Big Chief," but in what tribal language is unknown.[121] The camp was one of only two in Morgan County. (The other boy scout camp was at Nixon Grove in Deerfield Township.)

For more on the remarkable business activities and community leadership of Orton Dunn at Marietta and his commitment to boy scouting—holding both regional and national offices—see his death notice in the *Morgan County Democrat* (August 30, 1933, p. 1).

Sadly, his own son, "John E. Dunn, lost his life in a swimming accident at Devol's Dam on July 4, 1931." Orton Dunn died two years later.

---

[121] There is also a state lodge or inn in Canada with virtually the same name. I called the lodge and asked the clerk if he or anyone there knew in which Indian language "Endubonah" means "big chief." He said he did not know, but he and other employees had often wondered as well. (Appendix F, among others, is not within the time frame of the title of this document, but I thought it worth inserting lest the information be lost or forgotten. –RW)

Appendix G

Excerpts from
"NATHANIAL EVANS: A FRONTIER SOLDIER"
Elizabeth S. Cottle[122]
August 19, 1989

The Ohio D.A.R. Roster[123] states that Nathan Evans served as a private with New York troops under Colonel Van Schoonhoven. Also the *D.A.R. Patriot Index*[124] added that he married Mary Thomas and was a Sergeant in New York.

A further check found where the Evanses lived in Washington County, Ohio:

    1800 Census Waterford Township:
        Simeon Evans (household head)
            Nathanial Evans (living in same house)
    1807 Township Voting Lists:
        Marietta — Nathaniel Evans
        Roxbury — Luke Evens (sic)
                    Simeon Evens (sic)
        Waterford — Thomas Evans
    1810 Census:
        Roxbury — Simeon Evans
        Grandview —Anthony Evans, John Evans, Joseph Evans.
    1820 Census:
        Marietta — Mary Evens (sic)
        Roxbury — Samson Evans (probably misread, should be Simeon)
        Grandview — Anthony Evans, John Evans, Joseph Evans

Genealogist Barbara Covey of California then submitted ten cards on Nathaniel Evans from the National Archives in Washington, D.C., which place him on muster and payrolls at various times: Evans enlisted September 17, 1776, for the war in the 1st Independent Company, commanded by Capt. Robert Durkee from the town of

---

[122] *Tallow Light*, Vol. 20, No. 2, n.d., pp. 67-71. Condensed and edited by Richard Walker. This synopsis is included because Nathaniel Evans was half-Indian and his first (of nine children), Lois, born in Damascus, Wayne County, PA in 1764, wed Frederick Eveland [Jr.], who settled at pre-Stockport. (See pp. 34-6.) Nathaniel and his white wife Mary Thomas had nine children: Lois, Luke, Amy, Sally, Ziba, Simeon, Huldah, Samuel, and Hannah. It was Simeon Evans and his wife [Elizabeth Mellor or Miller, who wed June 19, 1799] who became prominent in the Roxbury, Ohio, community across the Muskingum from Big Bottom, the Buck Farm, and the Cheadle family stronghold. [N.B. The prolific, generous, and gracious author Elizabeth Cottle of Marietta was born February 19, 1908, and died December 18, 2011, age 103.]
[123] *Official Roster of the Soldiers of the American Revolution Buried in the State of Ohio*, by OSDAR (1929), p. 131.
[124] D.A.R. Patriot Index, 1966, p. 225.

Westmoreland, Connecticut. He was first stationed at Wyoming [in eastern Pennsylvania] when he began his service January 1, 1777, and was present in Millstone, Somerset County, New Jersey, the next month and [is] last listed on June 2, 1778. His outfit was regularly designated as Co. E, 4th Conn. Regt.

It appears that he and his company were fortunate to be absent from Wyoming on July 3, 1778, when the Indians and Tories attacked in a disastrous battle often called The Wyoming Massacre. Full reports on this battle may be found in histories of Wilkes-Barre, PA, which now occupies the site.

A more personal account of Nathaniel Evans' war service was produced many years later by his son Simeon who sent a letter dated Dec. 19, 1839 at Roxbury, Ohio, to Washington, D.C. seeking payment for the pension or bounty lands to which his father, who died in August 1808, would have been entitled.

One affidavit signed Sept 6, 1788, by William Hooker Smith, formerly Surgeon of the Garrison at Wyoming, certified that Evans was "a Pvt. Of the Continental Army under the command of Capt. Simeon Spalding . . . (after) an Expedition as far as the Genessee Country. [H]e was wounded on the return of the army to Wioming (sic). Evans was left in the Hospital unfit for Duty where he continued until the close of the War (and where) he became a useful man [working as a hospital aide]."

In another affidavit dated Oct. 6, 1788, Zebulon Butter, late Colonel, said that Evans served till the end of the war, and that in 1778 [he] was wounded by a rifle ball passing through his left thigh in a skirmish with the Indians.

The third affidavit of 1788 was from Simon Spalding, late captain of the Continental Army, who certified that Evans served during the war and was entitled to lands promised by Congress.

Also with the letter to Washington were sworn testimonials made in 1834 by two who had personally known Nathanial Evans. One statement was given in Morgan County [Ohio] by his [son-in-law] Frederick Eveland who mentioned Evans' hospital service until the close of the war. A second statement was made in Athens County by Job Phillips.

Simeon's request was turned down by the Bounty Land Office because official records show that Nathaniel Evans "did not serve as a soldier beyond the year 1778" and only those who served throughout the war were entitled to lands. These papers are preserved by the National Archives in the file on Invalid Pensions. . . .

From these papers we know that Nathaniel Evans remained at Wyoming [Pennsylvania] until the fall of 1788. He is not on Rufus Putnam's lists of Emigrants for 1788, 1789, or

1790. [However,] Nathaniel Evans and his sons Luke and Simeon arrived in Washington County, Ohio, in time to draw free 100-acre Donation lots given by the Ohio Company to actual settlers who would protect the approaches to Marietta. He is described as a laborer in Marietta in his deed from Rufus Putnam et. al., dated March 19, 1795.[125] His 100-acre Lot No. 33 was located in the South Branch of Little Wolf Creek Allotment, Range 10, Town 10, Sections 23 and 29. This was first in Waterford Township, then became part of Roxbury when that township was established in 1806, and is now in Watertown Township. The original survey lines and numbered townships remain constant even though the political names have changed.

Nathaniel Evans' lot was traversed by the south branch of Wolf Creek in such a way that most of his land was on the west side of the creek and a small piece was inconveniently on the east side. This small 15-acre portion was sold by Nath'l Evans of Waterford to David Wells on January 27, 1803, in a deed which was not recorded until December 18, 1812.[126] The 1810 Tax Duplicate lists the heirs of Nath'l Evans for 35 acres in the southwest corner of Lot 33 and Frederick Eveland [his son-in-law at pre-Stockport], but this was not recorded until the time of its sale to Abner Suber on March 13, 1813.[127]

Then on March 18, 1815, Sarah Evans, widow of Nathaniel Evans deceased and Samuel Evans, Luke Evans, Barna Sutliff, wife of Barna Sutliff, Jesse Scott and Anny Scott, wife of said Jesse Scott and Hannah Holt, all heirs of said Nathaniel Evans deceased deeded to Abner Suber all that part of Lot No. 33 not deeded to Abner Suber by Frederick Eveland.[128]

Family records name the nine children of Nathaniel Evans as Lois [of pre-Stockport], Luke, Anny [Amy?] Sally, Ziba, Simeon, Huldah, Samuel, and Hannah, five of whom are named in the above deed.

It is interesting that he turns out to be basically a Connecticut Yankee. He spent his adult life on three frontiers: The upper Delaware Valley where New York, Pennsylvania and New Jersey meet; the Wyoming Valley of Pennsylvania; and our own Mid-Ohio Valley.

---

[125] *Washington County Deeds*, Vol. 2, p. 108.
[126] *Washington County Deeds*, Vol. 12, p. 19.
[127] *Op. cit.*, Vol. 12, pp. 238, 240.
[128] *Op. cit.*, Vol. 14, p. 10.

Appendix H
"FREDERICK EVELAND OF STOCKPORT, OHIO"
Barbara L. Covey[129]
(1924-2012)
Rancho Palos Verdes, California
draft 1966

Frederick Eveland, Jr., of Stockport, Ohio, born in 1766, was a son of Frederick Eveland, Sr., who was the son of John Eveland, who was the son of Johann David Ifflandt. The 1850 Census of Randolph Grove Township, McLean County, Illinois, shows that he was age 84 when the Census was taken in October. He was living with his oldest daughter, Catharine, and her second husband, James Frisby. Frederick Eveland's occupation is shown as farmer and his birthplace as New Jersey.[130]

On August 14, 1766, Jr.'s father, Frederick, Sr., who later would serve in the 4th Consnecticut Regiment during the American Revolution, and Catrina Eveland, probably his wife, were witnesses in Walpeck, Sussex County, New Jersey, at the baptism of Catrina, daughter of Jan van gordern and Elizabeth van De Merken by Rev. Romine at the old Dutch Reformed Church.[131] This was about two months after the elder Eveland's making bond and qualifying as Administrator of his father's estate on 3 June 1766 in Sussex County, New Jersey. The deceased, John Eveland, had died intestate, circa October, 1765, "late of Newtown in the County of Sussex."[132]

In short, there is good evidence that our subject probably was born in Sussex County, New Jersey. There is a possibility that his mother was named Rosecrans, and the records of baptisms at the Walpeck Dutch Reformed Church in that era contain a large number of Rosecrans baptisms. Frederick and Catrina Eveland, however, did not have small Frederick baptized there. Where is unknown. They may not have been members of the Waleck Congregation for they appear in the records there only once, as noted above. Even for the baptism of Catrina van gorden, their name was originally spelled Edwart, a misspelling corrected later to "Evelant" by either Rev. Romine or by a transcriber.

William Lee and Antje Evelandt, probably a sister of the elder Frederick Eveland, Sr., had two children baptized at Walpeck, no witnesses [were] listed for the first baptism, but Jan van garden and Elizabeth van De Merken were witnesses at Leentie's baptism.

---

[129] Longtime teacher and indefatigable genealogist Barbara Lee (*nee* Harn) Covey was born 24 May 1924 at Galesburg, IL, and died 2 October 2012 at Torrance, California. She sent a draft of this essay to me several decades ago. *This appendix is her work and her words.* Whether she published it between 1966 and 2012 I do not know. I made minor edits and updates in 2023-24.
[130] State of Illinois Census, Randolph Grove Township, McLean County, 1850.
[131] *New York Genealogical and Biographical Record*, "Church Register of the Walpeck Congregation," Vol. 40 (1909), pp. 193-205 and 264-275, Vol. 41 (1910), pp. 28-43, 83-98, 200-15, and 345-67.
[132] New Jersey Archives.

Frederick Eveland, Sr., probably was accompanied by his family when he arrived on the Susquehanna River, 15 December 1771, to take land in the Connecticut-sponsored Susquehanna Purchase. A son, William C. Eveland, was born 18 February 1774, and another son, John, may have been born between Frederick, Jr., and William C. Eveland. Records of these births have not been found, but the evidence is plentiful that they were brothers.

They lived at Plymouth, Town[ship?] of Westmoreland, Connecticut, or in Shawney, Luzerne County, Pennsylvania, depending on whether they considered themselves "Yankees" or Pennamites, pioneering in this territory, ownership of which was bitterly disputed for a generation.

The first record found for the younger Frederick Eveland is a petition to the State of New York, dated February, 1783, and signed "at Westmoreland." His signature followed directly after his father's and was shown as "x Eveland, Frederick Junr." A footnote with the petition indicated that those signatures preceded by "x" were for minors.[133] This indicates that the younger man had not yet reached age 18, as he would before October 1783.

Of the 396 signers of this document, 58 had "x" before their names, showing that they were minors. These included Luke Evans, who would become Frederick Jr.'s brother-in-law a few years later. Luke Evans' signature followed his father's, Nathaniel Evans. Another minor with "x" before his name was Jonathan Frisbie, who signed after James Frisbie, and may have been the father of Frederick Eveland's eventual son-in-law, James Frisby.

The continual bellicose relationship between the pioneers from Pennsylvania and those from Connecticut had been solved in favor of the Pennsylvanians shortly before this petition. Accordingly, it said:

> We the subscribers hereby covenant and agree to and with each other, and jointly petition the Assembly of the State of New York for a tract of land situate on the waters of the Susquehanna and within the limits of said State, sufficient for us the subscribers, our families, and those who were Distressed and Drove from here by the savages in 1778; and also do hereby appoint Obadiah Gore our agent, with full power and authority to apply to the Governor and Senate of said State, or to the General Assembly, or to any Board within and for said State, proper to make application to for lands as aforesaid; and in our names and behalf to petition, &c., according to his best Descretion. In Testimony whereof we have hereunto set our hands at Westmoreland, this 12th day of February, 1783.

---

[133] Oscar Jewell Harvey, *A History of Wilkes-Barre*, Vol. III, 1929, p. 1314.

On 21 March, 1787, "Frederick Eveland of Shawney, Luzerne County, and formerly the property of the Proprietors of Connecticut." On 10 April 1787, "Frederick Eveland of Plymouth in the Susquehanna Purchase" conveyed to Benjamin Harvey of Plymouth certain lands on "Shawanese Flat." These two 1787 deeds suggest that the elder Frederick was selling his lands and planning to move to New York State, along with many of the original inhabitants under the Connecticut Susquehanna Company.[134]

It is clear that Frederick, Jr., and his wife, Lois Evans, accompanied his father to New York State, for their oldest son was born in New York State in 1787/88. He was named Nathaniel for his maternal grandfather, Nathaniel Evans, who, like Frederick, Sr., had served in the 4th Connecticut Regiment during the Revolutionary War.

The record does not show when or where Frederick, Jr. married Lois Evans, but it probably was "at Westmoreland" shortly after their father and Frederick, Jr., with others, signed the petition to New York State, dated 12 February 1783.

An estimate of the length of time that Frederick and Lois (*nee* Evans) lived in New York State can be made by looking at the birthplaces of their children as shown in the 1850 censuses: Nathaniel was born 1787/88 in New York[135]; Catharine 1789/90 in New York[136]; David in 1793/94 in New York[137]; and Moses in 1793/94[138]—*all* in New York state.

Catharine was probably named for her paternal grandmother, David for the progenitor of the family in the New World, and Moses for Lois' maternal grandfather, Moses Thomas. Two other children, Amy and John, are less easy to document as to birthplace since each had died before 1850.[139]

The date of their move to Ohio is unknown. It was long enough before 17 April 1797 for Frederick Eveland, Sr., to establish his residence in Belleprie [Belpre], "in the County of Washington and Territory of the United States north west of the River Ohio," before taking advantage of the offer of the Ohio Land Company of 100 acres of Donation Tract land free to any male 18 or over who would agree to carry a gun and protect the approaches to the Marietta settlement from the Indians. In a deed dated 17 April 1797, Rufus Putnam, Manasseh Cutler, Griffin Green, and Robert Oliver, "by virtue of the powers and in of the trust reposed in us," granted to Frederick Eveland of Belleprie one hundred acres of land

---

[134] Recorder of Deeds, Luzerne County, Pennsylvania.
[135] State of Illinois Census, Watertown Township, Fulton County, 1850.
[136] State of Illinois Census, Randolph Grove Township, Fulton County, 1850.
[137] State of Illinois Census, Liverpool Township, Fulton County, 1850.
[138] State of Indiana Census, Centre Township, Dearborn County, 1850.
[139] Because Amy Eveland married Daniel Dennis in 1815 and John Eveland married Harriet Newton in 1818, in Washington County, Ohio, they must have been born in 1800 or before. The location probably was Waterford Township, Washington County, because that is where Frederick and Lois (*nee* Evans) Eveland appear to have been living in 1804 when Nathaniel Evans sold them land.

"lying in Mile lot No. 21 of 22 of the Third Township in the Ninth Range surveyed agreeable to the Ordinance of Congress of the twentieth of May, 1785."[140]

There is no way to tell whether this was Frederick Senior, who had been married to Nancy Lee on 16 March 1797 by Josiah Munro, J.P.[141], or Frederick Junior and Lois (*nee* Evans) Eveland. However, on 25 July 1797, Frederick Eveland and Samuel Lee each sold one hundred acres of land to Dudley Woodbridge for $100. The description of Eveland's lot would indicate it was the one granted him in April; Samuel Lee was witness for this transaction. Samuel Lee's lot was identified as lying in Mile lot No. 78 of the fourth Township in the ninth Range. Frederick Eveland, in turn, was the witness.[142]

No other deeds of Donation Tract lands to a Frederick Eveland have been located, but various listings of those who received lands are available. One states:

> Little Wolf Creek Allotment: Amos Eveland, Frederick Eveland, Frederick Eveland Jr., and Nathaniel Evans.
> Rainbow Creek Allotment: Frederick Eveland, Jr., John Eveland.[143]

Other deeds of interest include the 17 April 1797 grant of 100 acres to John Eveland of Belleprie, probably the son of Frederick Sr. and a brother of Frederick Jr. This was in "Mile Lot No. 22 or 21 of the third Township in the 9th Range."

In September, 1797, John Eveland sold his one hundred acres to Dudley Woodbridge for $100. John Woodbridge, rather than an Eveland or a Lee, was the witness.[144]

On 20 February 1798, John Lawrence "of the City of New York (but) now in the City of Philadelphia," sold land in Marietta to Dudley Woodbridge for $200. (While no family connection is known, it is interesting to note that the senior Frederick Eveland's mother had been "the daughter of Hannis Lawrence." Hannis is a diminutive of Johannis or John.[145])

---

[140] Recorder of Deeds, Washington County, Ohio, Vol. 5, p. 459
[141] Bernice Graham and Elizabeth S. Cottle, *Washington County, Ohio Marriages 1789-1840*, Marietta, Ohio, July 4, 1976, p. 45.
[142] Recorder of Deeds, Washington County, Ohio, Vol. 5, pp. 866 and 869.
[143] See Verna Trayer (1942-2022), *Name Index for 'Stockport, Ohio, A Compendium of Historical Information,'* 1984.
[144] Recorder of Deeds, Washington County, Vol. 5, pp. 462 and 711.
[145] *Ibid.*, Vol. 5, p. 473.

On 24 January 1803, Haffield White sold 30 acres in the fifth Township tenth Range to Frederick Eveland of Washington County for $150. Nathaniel Evans was the witness, and this transaction may have involved Frederick Eveland, Jr., and his father-in-law.[146]

A year later, 14 January 1804, Nathaniel Evans of Waterford sold Frederick Eveland of Waterford "a certain piece of land lying and being situate in Waterford aforesaid and in that part thereof called Southwest Branch Allotment and in part of the Original Lot No. 33 . . . of the South west branch of Wolf Creek.[147] This deed was not recorded until 9 September 1813, after Eveland had sold the same parcel to Abner Suber on 17 March 1813.[148]

Nathaniel Evans "of Marietta" received his one hundred acres from Rufus Putnam, Manasseh Cutler, Griffin Green, and Robert Oliver on 9 March 1795. It was "in mile lot no. 23 of 29 in the fourth township and tenth range."[149] On 18 March 1815, Sarah Evans, "widow of Nathaniel Evans deceased," and other heirs of Nathaniel Evans were selling the remaining lands "minus that sold to Frederick Eveland" and Abner Suber.[150]

In 1800 a local census was taken of the Northwest Territory. [Ohio became a state in 1803 and the first U.S. Census of Ohio was taken in 1810, but the 1810 records were destroyed by fire, thus the U.S. Census in 1820, became "first" by default.] In that census only three Evelands were recorded: John in Roxbury Township, Nathaniel in Waterford Township, and Frederick in Wooster [now Watertown] Township.[151] Morgan County was legally erected on December 29, 1817. In the next decade the Ohio legislature created, shifted, and sometimes dissolved county and township boundaries. In the 1820 Ohio Census in Windsor Township, Morgan County, Ohio (which both gained and lost land from Washington and adjoining counties), five Eveland males are listed:

> John, born 1794-1804; Frederick, born pre-1775; Nathaniel, born 1775-94; Moses, born 1794-1804; and David, born 1775-94.[152]

These are clearly Frederick, Jr., and his sons. There is one unidentified male family member among the Evelands in the household of Nathaniel. At the same time in this early era, there were constant land transactions—wills, sales, forfeitures, grants, mergers, deaths, etc. After 1819 in Morgan County many land transactions involved Frederick Eveland, Jr., but not Frederick Eveland, Sr., the Revolutionary War veteran. Why not? In 1820 he was about age 80, but no longer lived in Ohio. He, along with relatives and in-laws, had

---

[146] *Ibid.*, Vol. 12, p. 420.
[147] *Ibid.*, Vol. 12, p. 238.
[148] *Ibid.*, Vol. 12 p. 240.
[149] *Ibid.*, Vol. 2, pp. 108-09.
[150] *Ibid.*, Vol. 14, pp. 110-12.
[151] See notes above.
[152] State of Ohio Census, Windsor Township. Morgan County, Ohio, 1820.

moved to Illinois. And before he died in Waynesville, Illinois, in 1838 he had even taken a new wife, Miss Brock!

> Frederick Eveland [Jr., was born in 1764 in Newbury, New Jersey, and died December 20, 1854, in Bloomington, Illinois. He wed in Tioga County, New York, in 1786 and subsequently brought his wife and their children from New York via Pennsylvania to Ohio and] settled where Stockport now is in 1811. They occupied a double log cabin, in one room of which he kept saloon, while his wife, a religious woman, lived and frequently had religious meetings in another room. Neither meddled with the affairs of the other, and they lived harmoniously together. Frederick's sons, Nathaniel, David, Moses, and John and several daughters, were also residents of the township. Nathaniel Lucas, a blacksmith by trade, settled in the same neighborhood in 1811.[153]

Amy Eveland, daughter of Frederick, Jr., and Lois (*nee* Evans) Eveland [at Stockport]—who had apparently been named for Lois' sister, Amy Anna (*nee* Evans) Scott—married Daniel Dennis on 16 April 1815. She became the mother of Sylvester and Amy Dennis. After she died, Daniel Dennis wed Cassandra Stump on 14 February 1819. Simeon Evans was Lois' [*nee* Evans] brother. Asa Cheadle, J.P., married John Eveland and Harriet Newton in 1818. "Opposite the site of the village of Stockport was Nathaniel Eveland, and next below, Samuel White. Asa White occupied the Silverheels Farm [after] Arthur Taggart [died]."[154]

"Nathaniel Eveland and William Hughes lived together on the farm [which was later owned by] Robert Henery 2nd. Hughes was a great bear hunter and he and his large black dogs were familiar figures in the woods for miles around."[155]

The only mention that Robertson's *History of Morgan County, Ohio* in 1886 makes of Nathaniel Evans, father of Lois (*nee* Evans) Eveland, is in connection with Evans' son Simeon. Perhaps, it sheds light on Lois' being such a religious woman that she could hold religious meetings in the same house where her husband was keeping saloon:

> Simeon Evans, or Grandfather Evans as he was familiarly known, was born in Orange County, New York, in 1776, and came with his father Nathaniel Evans, to Washington County [Ohio] in 1794. The family settled near Marietta [Belpre] and the elder Evans is buried in the Marietta cemetery. [See Appendix F.] Simeon Evans was one of the early pioneers of Windsor Township, Morgan County, Ohio, where he settled about 1796. He married Miss Elizabeth Mellor on June 16, 1799. The name of Evans is one

---

[153] Robertson, *History of Morgan County, Ohio*, 1886, p. 401. My inserts from other sources are given in brackets. N.B., Covey's quotation of Robertson's work on this page should sound familiar. It is the same as that which is quoted on p. 35 and referenced in footnotes #43 and #44. –RW.
[154] *Op. cit.*, 1886, p. 392.
[155] *Op. cit.*, 1886, p. 402.

familiar to everyone in the southern part of the county, where they are known as honest, intelligent, and upright people. Simeon, the progenitor of the family in Morgan County, was a fine type of the pioneer. He was a religious man and in the early days his house was known far and near as the "preaching place" for the Methodists . . . [156]

Decades later a number of Lois and Simeon's children were members of the Oakland Methodist Church, which was organized in 1854, although her name does not appear. As well, Lois Eveland does not appear among the January 11, 1818, organizers of the Windsor Baptist Church, although a "Sarah Evans" was one of the original 35 members. (She could have been either Nathaniel Evans' widow Sarah or Simeon Evans' daughter Sarah.) "First known as the First Baptist Church of Roxbury, its services were conducted for many years in private houses, schoolhouses, and barns."[157] Daniel Dennis, her son-in-law, is listed among the original 35 members, although Amy, his wife, is not.

Windsor Township had about 60 families when it was organized by the commissioners on July 7, 1819. Part of Windsor Township, Morgan County, had originally been in Roxbury Township, Washington County. The 33 eligible (male only) voters in July, 1819, included Frederick Eveland, Nathaniel Eveland, and Silvanus Newton, father-in-law of John Eveland, a son of Frederick and Lois (*nee* Evans) Eveland.[158] Why David and Moses Eveland, both old enough to vote in 1819, are not on the list, yet are in the Census of 1820 is unknown. Perhaps they had accompanied their uncle John to Illinois Territory, where a Moses Evlin (sic) and a John Evlin (sic) appear in the 1818 Illinois Census. In the household of Moses in Illinois were one white male and six "all others." John Evin's (sic) household had three white males and ten others![159]

By the time Morgan County was legally organized, four of Frederick and Lois (*nee* Evans) Eveland's children had married. Their Washington County marriages were:[160]

> 1. Nathaniel Eveland of Waterford wed Cynthia Scott of Waterford, 10 April, 1806, by Robert Oliver, J.P. (Cynthia Scott was Nathaniel's cousin, daughter of Jesse and Amy Anna [*nee* Evans] Scott.)
> 2. Russell Darrough of Waterford wed Catharine Eveland of Waterford, 10 April, 1806, by Robert Oliver, J.P.
> 3. Daniel Dennis wed Amy Eveland, 16 April 1815, by Thomas White, J.P., of Roxbury, Ohio.
> 4. John Eveland of Roxbury wed Hariett Newton of Roxbury, 21 April 1818, by Asa Cheadle J.P. Harriet Newton was the daughter of Silvanus and Elizabeth (*nee* Stacy) Newton.

---

[156] Robertson, *op. cit.*, 1886, p. 397.
[157] *Op. cit.*, 1886, p. 412.
[158] Walker, *op. cit.*, p. 57.
[159] *Illinois Census Returns*, Statistical Returns, Vol. III, Collections of the Illinois State Historical Library, edited by Margaret Cross Norton, Illinois State Library, Springfield, IL.
[160] Bernice Graham and Elizabeth Cottle, *Washington County, Ohio, Marriages, 1789-1840*, 1976.

In addition to these marriages, others which involved the Evelands include:

Levi Roberts of Roxbury to Lucy Eveland of Roxbury, 14 May 1812, by Timothy M. Gates, J.P. She was the oldest daughter of John and Elizabeth Eveland and a niece of Frederick Eveland at pre-Stockport. As well, John Eveland of Morgan County wed Elvira Walbridge of Washington County on 2 November 1838, by Rasellus Wood, J.P. Elvira may have been the daughter of Isaac Walbridge and Elizabeth Newton, oldest sister of Harriet Newton who married John Eveland on 21 April 1818. These were different John Evelands and the one who married in 1838 was likely the son of David and Nancy Newton, a third sister. It is an accepted fact among their descendants that brothers David and John Eveland married sisters Nancy and Harriet Newton. David, Jr., son of David and Nancy (*nee* Newton) Eveland was born 11 May 1816. There were two little boys in their household in 1820, the second probably was John.

Simeon Evans and Elizabeth Miller/Mellor were married on 16 June 1799 by Robert Oliver, J.P., who also officiated at the weddings of Nathaniel Eveland to Cynthia Scott and of Russell Darrough to Catharine Eveland on 10 April 1806.[161] A record of Moses Eveland's wedding to Dorothy Craig could not be found.

The Frederick Eveland born between 1810 and 1815, who married Margaret Hargus in Morgan County 3 September 1829, may have been a son of Nathaniel and Cynthia (*nee* Scott) Eveland.

The 1830 Census for Morgan County lists in succession, with only one intervening name [Sam Walters], Frederick and Lois (*nee* Evans) Eveland's three oldest sons:[162]

Nathaniel Eveland	2	born 1810-30, 1 born 1780-90.
Samuel Walters	3	born 1810-30, 1 born 1790-1800.
Moses Eveland	1	born 1810-30, 1 born 1790-1800.
David Eveland	2	born 1810-30, 1 born 1790-1800.

Much farther along in the Census and separated by a number of households—but still in Windsor Township, Morgan County—is Frederick Eveland, born 1760-70, and his wife born in same decade, whom we know was Lois Evans. Also listed are a male and female born 1800-10 who quite likely were John and Harriet (*nee* Newton) Eveland. The conclusive evidence that this is John and Harriet lies in the presence of five little boys, all under age ten. This can only be John and Harriet, now living with his parents. Next door was Elias Darrow, son of Catherine (*nee* Eveland) and Russell Darrough (sic).

---

[161] *Ibid*.
[162] Ohio Census, 1830, Windsor Township, Morgan County.

In this regard, Robertson's pre-Stockport overview is worth repeating:

> Frederick Eveland and his sons, David, Moses, and John, occupied the site of Stockport, and several brothers by the name of Lucas were also in this neighborhood prior to 1815. Further down [river] at an early period were Andrew Dennis, a Revolutionary War soldier, and his sons, Daniel, Samuel, Thomas, Andrew, and Uriah; Daniel Coleman and Jacob Nulton; Asa Cheadle, Simeon Nott, and Simeon Evans, all very early.[163]

On 5 July 1830, John Eveland died. Our [i.e., Barbara Covey's] family tradition has been that he was a boat builder and died in an accident, but no record has been found to prove it.

On 22 November 1833, Harriet, John's widow, was reprimanded by the Court of Common Pleas for having

> neglected and refused to support and maintain [Frederick Eveland and his wife] from the time of the death of ... John, the husband of said Harriet and father of the other defendants [elsewhere identified as Joel, Abner, Johnson, Chandler, and Jonas Eveland, sons of John and Harriet (*nee* Newton) Eveland] until the time of this decree.[164]

The court noted that John had received from Frederick a deed for the land on which they lived together, that John "entered into the possession and occupancy of said land and so continued until his death and that said Frederick and wife resided with and were supported by said John in fulfillment of the terms and stipulations in said Bill mentioned until the death of the said John as aforesaid."[165]

The court ordered that Harriet and the other defendants, heirs of John Eveland, provide for, maintain, and support Frederick and his wife during each of their lives "with such boarding, lodging, washing clothes, and others things as may be necessary for their comfort."[166] And Frederick Eveland was directed, "while so supported," to do "what reasonable labor he was able to do on said land." But on 17 March 1836, this judgment was reversed and Frederick was ordered to pay court costs of $7.42 and one half cents.[167]

On 29 April 1835, Harriet brought suit against Moses and David Eveland, saying that she could not pay the debts left her by John. She claimed that he had owned a one-third interest in a saw

---

[163] Charles Robertson, *History of Morgan County, Ohio*, 1886, p. 401.
[164] Minutes of the Court of Common Pleas, Vol. C, Courthouse, McConnelsville, Ohio, p. 33.
[165] *Ibid.*, p. 34.
[166] *Ibid.*
[167] *Ibid.*

mill located on Bald Eagle Creek, and that they owned the remainder. She now wanted to sell it in order to pay her debts. Also, she said that John had owned "the East end & half of lot No. 1058 in Section 32, Township 9, Range 11, in Morgan County, containing 160 acres,"[168] which she also wanted to sell. She asked the court to appoint appraisers of these properties, and a later entry shows that the land was judged to be worth $112.50, the third of the saw mill at $225.[169] One family tradition states that, after John's accidental death at age 30, Harriet farmed out her sons to various families while she got her finances in order. It is unknown which sons went to which families, nor the specific finances which Harriet, only age 26 when widowed, had to solve.

In the 1840 Census, Harriet and her five sons were listed together, still living in Windsor Township, Morgan County, Ohio, but still at a considerable distance from David and Moses, as in 1830. Harriet's next-door neighbor in 1830, Elias Darrow, no longer occupied the house next door to her in 1840. Perhaps he and his mother, Catherine (*nee* Eveland) Darrow Frisby, had already moved to Illinois where they settled near her grandfather, old Frederick Eveland of the Revolutionary War, who had died in 1838. Frederick and Lois (*nee* Evans) Eveland are not shown in the 1840 Ohio Census.[170]

By 1850 the picture had changed. The censuses for DeWitt and McLean Counties in Illinois are filled with people who were–or would become in successive generations–related to the Evelands. Of particular note, James Frisby, age 64, born in Pennsylvania, with real estate valued at $6000, was living in Randolph Grove Township, McLean County. With him and his wife, Catharine, age 60, born in New Jersey, and her father, Frederick Eveland, age 84, born in New Jersey![171]

Elias Darrow and his family were located in DeWitt County, a part of which had been set off from McLean County.[172]

David Eveland, age 59, born in New York, can be located in 1850 in Liverpool Township, Fulton County, Illinois. With him was his wife, Nancy (*nee* Newton), age 52, born in Massachusetts. Three of Harriet (*nee* Newton) Eveland's sons were living together in Liverpool Township, at not too great a distance from them.[173] The Mortality Tables for that year reveal that Harriet, too, had been there at her death, the spring of 1850. Moses Eveland, age 56, born in New York, was living in Aurora, Centre Township, Dearborn County, Indiana, with his wife, Dorothy, age 50, born in Virginia.[174]

Ben Root of Ottumwa, Iowa, a descendant of Frederick and Lois (*nee* Evans) Eveland, sent

---

[168] The boundary stake at the southeast corner of narrow east-west 160-acre rectangular Lot #1058, is also the northwest corner stake of the corporation limit of present-day Stockport, Ohio.
[169] Minutes of the Court of Common Pleas, Vol. C, Courthouse, McConnelsville, Ohio, p. 331.
[170] State of Ohio Census, Windsor Township, Morgan County, 1840.
[171] State of Illinois Census, Randolph Grove Township, McLean County, 1850.
[172] State of Illinois Census, DeWitt County, 1850.
[173] State of Illinois Census, Liverpool Township, Fulton County, 1850.
[174] State of Indiana Census, Aurora, Centre Township, Dearborn County, Indiana.

additional information [to Barbara Covey], as researched by his mother, which indicates that Frederick Eveland's dates were **1764-1854** and Lois Evans' were **1768-1849** and that they were "buried on the Brock farm, in Bloomington, Illinois,"[175] which indicates it was the same cemetery as his father, the Revolutionary War veteran. Apparently, neither grave has a marker.

A biography of Greenbury H. Eveland (son of Abner and Betsy [*nee* Ackerson] Eveland, son of John and Harriet [*nee* Newton] Eveland, son of Frederick and Lois [*nee* Evans] Newton) says,

> Going back in the paternal line three generations, we come to Frederick Eveland. . . . He emigrated to Ohio, taking his place among the frontiersmen of Morgan County. He bought a tract of timber land on the banks of the Muskingum River, from which he gave each of his children a farm. After having lived there many years, he came to Illinois, and spent his last years with a daughter near Bloomington. He was a great hunter, successful in trapping and killing various kinds of game that were abundant and finding a ready sale for the furs which he secured.[176]

---
[175] Ben and Barbara Root, 434 South Willard, Ottumwa, Iowa.
[176] *Portrait and Biographical Album of Fulton County, Illinois*, Biographical Publishing Company, Chicago 1890, p. 614.

Appendix I

Names and Addresses of Residential Telephone Subscribers in 1993 Listed with Stockport, Ohio, Telephone Prefix 614-559

and

74 Others with a Stockport Mail Route Address Listed under Watertown Prefix 614-749 [N = 50], Beverly Prefix 614-984 [N = 23], or Barlow Prefix 614-678 [N=1][177]

A

Abel, Mike North St
Abrams, Kathryn 5803 Twp Rd 22
Adams, J D Madison St
Adams, Oneita St Rt 266
Adams, Robert & Dorothy North St.
Addington, Robert E Co Rd 2
Addis, Carl 1008 St Rt 376
Addis, Juanita F & Jeff A 1090 St Rt 376
Adkins, Don North St
Adkins, Fred Co Rd 2
Adkins, Kevin Broadway St
Adkins, Richard L Co Rd 2
Ahartmarvin, A Twp Rd 39
Albert, Karen Twp Rd 151
Allberry, William North St.
Allberry, William E. Jackson St.
Anderson, B E 6430 St Rt 792
Andrews, Joyce Co Rd 2
Ankeny, Jack Twp Rd 179
Ankrom, Morris C Twp Rd 934
Antill, Ida M 2340 S Patterson Ridge Rd SE
Ash, Richard 4260 Olney Run Rd

B

Bachelor, C A R D 3
Bachelor, Ray & Faye Main & Tieber
Bailey, Lina 1216 Main
Balderson, Tommy Twp Rd 39
Ball, Bonnie Melissa 4000 Twp Rd 22
Bankes, Maynard R North St
Barrett, Richard N 4800 E Roxbury Rd SE
Barrett, Virginia R 4700 E Roxbury Rd SE
Bebout, Gene Co Rd 6
Bebout, James Franklin St
Bebout, R D Co Rd 6
Bebout, Randy & Lori Twp Rd 181
Bebout, Roger E 38 Big Oak Rd
Beck, Albert North St
Beck, Robert & Dianna Co Rd 66
Behymer, Dorothy Twp Rd 22
Behymer, Edward Twp Rd 22
Berry, Dennis St Rt 266
Best, Kathy & Brian 1951 St Rt 266 SE
Bishop, C R Main St
Blackstone, Clark V 2820 Sycamore Ln
Blind, E D 3605 E Blind Rd SE
Blind, John Morgan Co Rd 18
Blind, Phillip Morgan Co Rd 18
Blind, Ruth Co Rd 2
Blind, Shelly St Rt 792
Blind, Tom Morgan Co Rd 206
Bole, Chester Broadway St
Bonar, James Co Rd 2

---

[177] *United Telephone of Ohio Directory*, February, 1993. N.B.: The United Telephone of Ohio often misspelled the surname "Olney" as "Oney." I have corrected it herein. —RW

Bookman, Charles & Brenda Main St
Boone, James & Deborah Twp Rd 181
Branscomb, Thomas D Co Rd 2
Brandon, Frances Co Rd 2
Brokaw, C W North St
Brokaw, Donald Co Rd 6
Brooks, Daniel T 4040 E River Rd
Brown, B L Washington Co Rd 18
Brown, Ray Co Rd 2
Browning, B L Washington Co Rd 18
Broyles, C B Twp Rd 39
Broyles, Richard Cleveland Av
Brunner, Larry T 5662 E Olney Run Rd SE
Buchanan, Jerry 118 Southmore Rd SE
Burfield, Robert Broadway St
Burfield, Timothy 3450 S St Rt 792
Burgett, Betty J Main St
Burt, Dwight & Kay Co Rd 2
Burt, Dwight L Palmer Twp Rd 6
Burt, Leland Palmer Twp Rd 6
Byers, James A Twp Rd 602
Byers, Michael G 2449 St Rt 266

C

Cain, David B. 1780 Broadway
Cain, Dean 3001 S Ash Rd SE
Cain, Glen Twp Rd 22
Cain, Joe Twp Rd 22
Cain, Ronald 4525 Twp Rd 22
Calendine, B M North St
Calendine, Jerry Main St
Campbell, Bill & Lori Co Rd 61
Campbell, John J Co Rd 92
Campbell, Rickey C Co Rd 92 Malta
Carroll, Simeon 2524 Sycamore Ln
Caruso, Henry E St Rt 266 S
Casto, Robert C Co Rd 61
Chandler, Carl Washington Co. Rd 18
Cheadle, Columbus R.D. 3
Cheadle, Columbus, Jr. Morgan Co. R.D. 3
Cheadle, Terry Joe 3105 Tieber Rd.
Cheadle, Tim & Crystal Rd 3
Chandler, Carl Washington Co. Rd. 18
Chew, Lynn 1077 Co Rd 6

Clawson, Nina J 333 Main St
Clum, T D Main St
Cochran, James L Twp Rd 22
Coler, Ron Broadway St
Collins, Joe H Kosky Dr
Coleman, Brent and Diana Co Rd 69
Coleman, Daniel St Rt 676
Coleman, Donald B St Rt 676
Coleman, Gary Twp Rd 88
Coleman, James S. Morgan Co Rd 88
Coleman, Linda and Jerry 7188 S Dale Rd
Coleman, Richard A. R D 3
Coleman, Ronald R D 3
Coleman, Warrior Stockport
Cooper, Darla St. Rte 676
Conner, see Bachelor
Cooley, R L North St
Coonrod, A St Rt 376
Cooper, Jerry C 2497 S Patterson Ridge Rd
Cooper, John E Twp Rd 23
Cooper, Opal Mrs 6162 S Dale Rd SW
Cooper, Richard A 5570 S Dale Rd SE
Core, Charles J 3950 Twp Rd 38
Covey, M C 2950 Sycamore Ln
Cozzens, George Wash. Co 18
Creighton, David & Lynn Co Rd 2
Creighton, John Co Rd 2
Creighton, Patrick Co Rd 2
Crow, John H. St Rt 266
Cunningham, Brian K Co Rd 18
Cunningham, Chester N Tieber Rd
Cunningham, Elmer St Rt 792
Cunningham, Goldie Mrs. North St
Cunningham, Kenneth Co Rd 69
Cunningham, Marc & Jill Broadway
Cunningham, Steve M Co Rd 2

D

Dailey, Lori St Rt 376
Danielson, Glen L 1646 Co Rd 2
Davis, Cecil Co Rd 6
Davis, Dean A Co Rd 6
Davis, Dwight Co Rd 36
Davis, Glenn Elmwood St

Davis, Harley L Co Rd 36
Davis, James & Susan Market St
Davis, Jeff Co Rd 36
Davis, Kate Co Rd 36
Davis, Keith Co Rd 36
Davis, Ralph Co Rd 179
Davis, Virgil S Tieber Rd
Dawson, Estel Market St
Diller, Marion St Rd 266
Dille, Jeremy S & Pam S Market St
Dille, Verlyn 617 S McCoy Ridge Rd SE
Dobbins, Wayne & Mary Broadway St
Dotson, Edward T St Rd 792
Dovenbarger, Roy Co Rd 6
Drobrina, Edward 1587 Co Rd 92
Drobrina, Paul J. III Twp. Rd 176
Dunn, Bruce G 2272 St Rt 266
Dupre, Charles Rt 2 Box 30
Duvall, Rodney A 1798 S Point Lookout Rd SE

E

Earhart, L E Twp Rd 23
Earich, Roger L Main St
Eckert, C L 3825 E Johnson Ridge Rd
Eckert, Daniel North St
Eckert, Don Co Rd 60
Eckert, Edwin Co Rd 2
Eckert, Mike Main St.
Eckert, Philip D Twp Rd 38
Eddleblute, David Tieber Rd
Eddleblute, Delbert St Rt 792
Edwards, Frank H 2340 E River Rd
Elliott, Joseph S 5801 St Rd 79
Ellis, Marilyn E 125 Main
Ellis, Sylvia Main St
Epling, Kenneth 3887 St Rt 792 SE
Erwin, Charles 333 Main
Ewart, Larry & Kelly 1635 Main

F

Faires, B E 1820 North
Faires, Frank R "Hank" 3015 Franklin St.
Faires, Helen Main St

Farnsworth, James A 5880 Rt 3
Farnsworth, James E Main St
Ferrebee, James Tieber Rd
Fitch, Don North St
Fleischer, M 2556 Sycamore Ln
Ford, S Twp Rd 22
Foreman, William Main St
Fountoukis, Paul 3575 Lighter Ridge Rd
Fox, R P 2555 S Bald Eagle Rd
Freeland, C S North St
Fritzsche, Robert E 2675 Sycamore Ln
Frye, Ellen I 1920 Broadway
Frye, Garnett Main St
Fryer, Harold J Twp Rd 602
Fryman, Richard D & Betty L North St.
Fulmer, Mary Main St

G

Gage, A J Co Rd 2
Gage, Daniel M Madison St
Gage, Joe Co Rd 2
Gage, John G St Rt 792
Garner, Betty 2274 E River Rd
Garrett, Russell D 2296 E St Rt 266 SE
George, Duane Cleveland Av
Gheen, Carlos Co Rd 92
Gheen, David Twp Rd 18
Gheen, Elmer Co Rd 69
Gilbreath, Larry D 1790 S Point Lookout Rd SE
Gillespie, Marion 720 E Daugherty Rd SE
Gohring, Donnie Co Rd 6
Gohring, Gary & Ruth 1590 Main
Gohring, Jonathan Main St
Goss, Lucille St Rt 266
Gotschall, Bill 4990 Roxbury Rd SW
Graham, Brent & Sherry 1888 St Rt 376 S
Graham, Robert L St Rd 266
Guinn, Greg St. Rd 676
Grandy, Robert Sycamore Ln
Gray, John H 2588 Sycamore Ln
Greuey Lester "Doc" & Bonnie Co Rd 6
Groah, David Twp Rd 176
Groah, Marie H Twp Rd 176

Grove, Robert & Amy North St
Guinn, Chuck & Beth Franklin St
Guinn, J L Broadway
Guinn, Roger Co Rd 60

H

Hager, Kathy & Matt 444 Main St
Haley, John C RD 2
Hall, Donald 3511 St Rt 792
Hall, Tom 605 Riverview Lane
Hambel, "Jim" 2500 Twp Rd 181
Hambel, Mike Co Rd 36
Hambel, Wendell Co Rd 36
Haney, Nancy 1234 Main St
Hankinson, William J 2345 Sycamore Ln
Hanson, Arthur & Thelma 5210 E Hanson Rd SW
Hanson, Edgar W Co Rd 36
Hanson, George W 5210 Hanson Rd SW
Hanson, Marcus St Rt 376
Hanson, Steve & Alice 695 E Shrivers
Harkins, W H St Rt 266
Harlow, Donald 2601 E River Rd
Harlow, Kenneth L North St
Harlow, Lyle E St Rt 792
Harlow, Peggy Main
Harmon, Ted & Betty Market St
Harper, Ralph S St Rt 792
Harra, Ray RD 3
Harris, Gerald 2354 Sycamore Ln
Harris, Jerry St Rt 376
Harry, Gary W 669 Riverview Ln
Hatch, Mae 3151 Twp Rd 37
Hart, Blain St Rt 266
Hartleben, Bobby RD 3
Hartleben Fred RD 3
Hatfield, Sam North St
Haught, Denver P Co Rd 6
Hayes, William T North St
Hays, John T Jr Twp Rd 181
Hegele, Budd & Nancy S Point Lookout Rd SE
Hemkes, E S 3151 Twp Rd
Hemkes-Ross, Norvel M 3151 Twp Rd 37

Herbst, Carl Vern Main St
Hickman, Lula 1210 Main
Hill, Wilbur D Co Rd 2
Hoffman, L St Rt 266
Holland, Donald C & Barbara Co Rd 66
Holland, Donald S St Rt 792
Hollett, Evelyn Broadway St
Holtz, Wayne 2833 S SR 266
Hook, Bryant St Rt 266
Hook, I Hancock St
Hook, John Co Rd 2
Hook, Melvin & Mary Beth St Rt 266
Hooper, Leroy St Rt 266
Hooser, Joda SR 266
Hoover, Leslie D SR 266
Hopkins, George Twp Rd 602
Horner, Ina F St Rt 792
Horner, Jack 1775 South St
Horner, Jerry Twp Rd 46
Horner, Ray R Twp Rd 689
Horner, Robert M Washington St
Houston, William O Twp Rd 602
Howe, Leslie F 2900 Sycamore Ln
Huck, Paul N Twp Rd 1034
Huffman, Darrell E 2050 Huffman Ln
Humphrey, David Main St
Hurst, Richard E Jr 2455 Ervin Ln
Hutchinson, Charles K North St

J

James, Jeff & Brenda Main St
James, Judith L Market St
James, Tim Co Rd 61
Jarvis, David A 6289 St Rt 792
Jarvis, David W Co Rd 87
Jasper, Dennis L 2425 Ervin Ln
Jewell, James & Jean 5 Kosky Dr
Johnson, Larry D 1412 S St Rt 376 SE
Jones, Herbert J St Rt 266
Jordan, Cecil 52 Broadway
Jordan, Richard & Nancy Broadway St
Junn, Edward Twp Rd 47
Junn, Leo D North St

K

Kachner, Curt F 1490 Co Rd 2
Keffer, Cleo 3rd St
Keffer, Dan South St
Keffer, Eddie Twp Rd 22
Kern, Weir Broadway St
Kilbarger, Emanuel L 3084 Co Rd 61
Kidder, Wallace Washington CR 18
Kincaid, Tim Co Rd 17
Kirkbride, Cheryl D 3860 Johnson Ridge Rd
Kirkpatrick, R & H Co Rd 36
Konkler, James J 1950 Broadway
Konkier, James & Kim Market St
Korting, William South St
Kosky, Julius J St Rt 266
Kosky, Stephen 2528 St Rt 266
Kovacs, Thomas J 2601 E River Rd
Kraps, Frederick RD 3
Krigbaum, Kenneth Co Rd 6
Kuder, Charles D 2880 Sycamore Ln

L

Lamb, Anna C Main St
Lane, Stanley Main St
Lauer, R C 3515 S St Rt 266
Lautter, Mark 2660 St Rt 376
Laychak Michael G 1121 S Bailey Ridge SE Malta
Lee, Frank RD 3
Leonard, Burl Twp Rd 688
Leonard, Dorothy M 1232 Main
Lilly, Carlos L. St Rt 676
Lindeberg, John 2444 Ervin Ln
Linscott, Bruce & Lola Main St
Littlefield, Cliff B Union St
Loar, Sylvia J Main St
Locke, James F Market St
Locke, P B Market St
Lohr, D M 3690 Twp Rd 22
Lorenz, Donald C St Rt 676
Lowers, Pamela R 902 St Rt 266 E
Lowers, Roscoe & Kathleen Twp Rd 39
Lowther, David & Jill 3772 E Olney Run Rd SE
Lowther, Lloyd D Columbus St

M

Malcolm, Jeanne 2795 S Ash Rd SE
Manning, Everett Mrs Main St
Manning, Floyd Cleveland Av
Manning, Kevin Main St
Matson, Forrest W 7000 S Matson Rd SW
Matson, Timothy R Twp Rd 178
Maxwell, Francis L 3020 St Rt 376
Maxwell, Robert E & Diane 3689 S McCoy Ridge Rd SE
Mayle, Floyd Co Rd 2
Mayse, James and Vicki St Rd 266
McAtee, Dale & Anita 3111 Big Bottom Ln
McBride, Roger D 1750 Cleveland Av
McCain, Loren 2280 Sycamore Ln
McClaskey Bobby 531 Riverview Dr
McClelland, B & R 4030 S River Rd
McCoy, Harry B Broadway St
McCoy, Kenneth A Cleveland Av
McCoy, Tim St Rt 376
McDaniel, Kenneth 1693 St Rt 376
McElfresh, Ernest Main St
McGee, Bill 554 Broadway
McGee, Loretta RD 3
McGirr, D South St
McGrath, Bryan S Main
McGrath, Charles Main St
McGrath, Robert T North St
McGrath, Thomas 1218 Main
McGrew, Donald Twp Rd 22
McGrew, Elsie Twp Rd 22
McGrew, Howard 3794 S Lick Run Rd
McGrew, Howard Jr Co Rd 17
McGrew, Richard Twp Rd 22
McGrew, Robert Twp Rd 47
McGrew, Rodney G Broadway St
McKibben, Ray Main St
McKibben, Ray & Barb 4411 Lickrun Rd SE
McKnown, William E Co Rd 66
McLean, Don 617 Daugherty Rd SE
McLein, Hershell 4070 St Rt 266
McQuaid, Arthur L Twp Rd 602
McVeigh, Hobart Twp Rd 181

Medley, Dion R Broadway St
Metcalf, Nellie Broadway St
Metheney, Linda and Gary D Cr Rd 69
Miller, Daniel J Twp Rd 37
Miller, Donald V St Rt 266 Kosky Dr
Mills, Chester Main St
Mills Frank R & Frances North St
Mills, Helen K Main St
Minor, Eva Twp Rd 150
Monroe, Tommie RD 3
Moon, Floyd E 15 Kosky Rd
Moore, Larry Co Rd 69
Moore, Steve and Rhonda St Rt 676
Morris, Earl E North St
Morrow, Deane 303 N Taylor Hollow Rd NE
Motz, Hugh Church St
Mugg, John W & Ethel 2300 E St Rt 266 SE
Mullen, Carl E & Darlene A Co Rd 61
Mummey, Francis Co Rd 36
Mummey, Gary Co Rd 35
Murphy, Mark 3594 E Olney Run Rd SE
Muse, Donald J Rosewood St
Muse, Jerry A St Rt 266
Musser, Dale A Co Rd 2
Myers, Robert & Lynn 3175 Madison
Myers, Sam Elmwood St

N

Nelson, Steve Washington CR 18
Newland, Edna Co Rd 2
Newsom, Frank 2019 S Riverview Rd SE Malta
Newton, Glenn North St
Nolan, Vivian St Rd 676
Norman, Steven 2461 E Hooksburg Rd SE

O

O'brien David & Becky 4620 Lightner Ridge Rd
Oiler, Richard St Rt 266
Oiler, Robert Market St
Oliver, Donald L North St
Ormiston, Vance Main St

Orr, J L 3135 Tieber Rd

P

Palmer, Betty St Rd 266
Parent, Ernie & Judy Twp Rd 602
Paramiter, Richard D & Kim Co Rd 36
Parsons, Fay 1730 S Bailey Ridge Rd SE
Patterson, Brady 3315 3rd St
Patterson, Lucille Madison St
Pauley, Robert R D 2
Paxton, James R Twp Rd 178
Payne, Stanley T Co Rd 87
Pettibone, Vonda L Market St
Pierce, Micky Main St
Pierdinock, June St Rt 376
Pierson, Agnus M 3566 Market St
Pinkerton, Joe & Lisa 5720 St Rt 792
Pitchford, James G 2630 Sycamore Ln
Pohlman, Conrad A Twp Rd 350
Polito, James Wash. C R 18
Pollock, James Co Rd 61
Ponchak, Mike & Linda K. 5290 Twp Rd 46
Porter, Chester 1229 S McCoy Ridge Rd SE
Porter, Dixie St Rt 376
Porter, Donald 750 Geddes Rd
Porter, James Jr Twp Rd 893
Porter, Michael Co Rd 61
Powell, David W 2481 E St Rt 266
Powell, Sam Co Rd 6
Price, Kenneth North St
Pronio, James A Co Rd 87 Rt 3
Pryor, Donald J & Debbie St Rt 792
Pugh, Dale H Wash. Co Rd 206
Pugh, Glen, RD 3
Pugh, Kay [Stockport Rt.]
Pugh, Randy RD 3
Pugh, Rodney Washington CR 18
Pugh, Ruth Palmer Twp Rd 18
Pugh, Wayne Palmer Twp Rd 18

Q

Queen, Michael R 4511 S Lightner Ridge Rd
Quick, Robert L St Rt 266 E
Quinn, G W 2523 St Rd 266 SE

R

Raines, Carl 1976 S McCoy Ridge Rd
Raines, Clarence Co Rd 6
Ramhoff, Harry RD 2
Reed, Cecil W & Ann 1643 S Bailey Ridge Rd
Reed, Marshall Franklin St
Richards, Robert R Twp Rd 602
Richards, Ronald Co Rd 66
Riffle, L C 2808 Sycamore Ln
Riffle, Larry C Twp Rd 180
Ring, H M Main St
Rippey, Carl Co Rd 36
Roberts, Douglas Tieber Rd
Roberts, J Market St
Roberts, James R South St
Robinson, Colleen Co Rd 60
Robinson, Gary & Annette 2770 Johnson Ridge Rd
Robinson, Kevin & Kim St Rt 792
Robinson, Richard RD 2
Rodenbucher, Francis Co Rd 2
Rodgers, Ernest St Rt 266
Roe, Kenneth & Barbara 4427 Hanson Hill Rd
Ross, Marvin J RD 3
Ross, Russell J. RD 3
Rowland, David North St
Russell, Carl 1227 S Point Lookout Rd SE

S

Sampson, Johnny Sr Co Rd 2
Sands, Marty 4990 Roxbury Rd SW
Savage, M L North St
Schaad, Chris 7109 Co Rd 18
Schaad, Cynthia M 500 S McCoy-Ridge Rd
Schaad, John P Twp Rd 151
Schaad, John Sr Twp Rd 150
Schilling, Thomas Windsor Twp Rd 690
Schleith, Michael 2590 Twp Rd 181
Schultz, Norma St Rt 266
Scott, Gary & Norma J Twp Rd 22
Scott, Kenneth L Co Rd 60
Scott, Norma J Market St
Sealock, Dorian Main St
Sealock, Greg Twp Rd 181
Searl, John & Tammy Main St
Searles, Freeman Main St
Secoy, Roy L N Washington
Seibel, Charles W. RD 2
Seibel, Charles & Joy Co Rd 36
Severt, Evert R Co Rd 60
Sharp, William H St Rt 376
Sheets, Stanley 59 North
Shepard, Alden Co Rd 60
Sherman, Bonnie R Twp Rd 178
Sherman, Larry & Lena Co Rd 6
Sherman, Randy 2373 Olney Run Rd
Sherman, Virgil 774 S McCoy Ridge Rd
Shriver, Rodney L Co Rd 36
Shriver, Shane & Nikki   Market St
Shuster, Donald Twp Rd 22
Shuster, Mike Tieber Rd
Shuster, Mike Broadway St
Shuster, Richard 1819 Co Rd 36
Shuster, Roger 4416 Olney Run Rd
Shuster, William 1770 Point Lookout Rd
Simms, Joseph F Jr 3340 S St Rt 376
Slowter, John Broadway St
Smith, Alvis W Jr   Palmer Twp Td[?] 737
Smith, Charles F North St
Smith, Esta Rosewood St
Smith, John D Palmer Twp. Td[?] 737
Smith, Robert & Dorothy 2868 Sycamore Ln
Smith, Sam 3031 E Hooksburg Rd SE
Smith, Steven M St Rt 266
Smith, Tami S Broadway St
Snodgrass, James R St Rd 266
Sohrenssen, Kimberly M Main St
Soulsby, William T Kosky Dr
South, Dale St Rd 376
Spaulding, B L Kosky Dr
Spencer, F B 16 Kosky Dr
Spencer, Gene 2239 S Bald Eagle Rd SE
Spencer, James A Co Rd 42
Spencer, Raymond L Main St
Spencer, Richard 1440 Twp Rd 39

Spencer, Susie Tieber Rd
Sprouse Jim & Betty Co Rd 2
Stager, Dan 2885 Kefer Rd SE
Starling, Loyd F St Rt 792
Starling, Ronald Co Rd 2
Staskevich, Bernard B Franklin St
Stephens, Thomas Co Rd 2
Stewart, Randy 2359 Sr 266 SE
Stiers, Duane E Co Rd 60
Stiers, Jerry & Sandra 3599 Co Rd 60
Still, George Broadway St
Straten, David & Norma Kosky Dr
Streight, Michael 1541 Streight Ln
Strohl, James R 150 N Taylor Hollow Rd NE
Strohl, Joseph E & Jennifer L 110 Taylor Hollow Rd S
Stroud, Sue 3160 Tieber Rd
Suhoski, Albert Co Rd 92 Malta
Suhoski, Anthony Co Rd 92 Malta
Sullivan, Dick & Joy [SR] 266 Kosky
Swain, Jean Broadway St
Swain, Mark D Broadway St
Sweet, Lloyd R 902 St Rt 266 E
Swicegood, Jack R Co Rd 2 Malta

T

Tabler, M M 372 St Rt 376
Taylor, Roger A 4221 S Lick Run Rd
Tegge, Charles 3020 Ruhaca
Teter, Charles E Back St
Teter, Harry H 444 Main St
Teter, Mary & Melissa 444 Main St
Thomas, Wanda L North St
Thompson, Shirley 5200 E Hanson Rd
Thornhill, Carl J 4593 S Lightner Ridge Rd
Tompkins, Dwight H Co Rd 2
Tompkins, Rick 5300 Olney Run Rd SE
Totman, Donna Broadway St
Travis, Debbie D Market St
Travis, Randy J Market St
Travis, Richard & Cindy North St
Travis, Ronald Co Rd 61
Treadway, Jerald L & Betty B Co Rd 60
Treadway, L E 1208 Main

Treadway, James H 1360 S Bailey Ridge Malta
Troiano, Larry Co Rd 66
Turner, Carl R & Peggy Wash. CR 18
Turner, Claude A 4777 E J Ross Ln
Turner, Garry W 3511 Lookout Point Rd
Tuten, Richard R. Sr Rd 266
Tuttle, Ralph Twp Rd 18
Tuttle, Robert St Rt 792
Tuttle, Robert L, Jr 3350 E Olney Run Rd SE

U

Uncles, Billie 1891 South
Unrue, John W 1810 School

V

Valentine, Bonnie 1729 Co Rd 42
Valentine, Charles 2403 Ervin Ln
Vandine, Connie Co Rd 22
Vickers, James 3500 S Market
Voland, Les 379 St Rt 266
Voland, Walter 370 St Rt 266
VonVille Eugene P 2545 S Bald Eagle Rd

W

Wagoner, L G North St
Waite, Bernard C Jr St Rt 792
Waite, Joe & Darla St Rt 792
Waite, William S. St R. 676
Walker, Charles Jackson St
Walker, Grace Mrs Main St
Walker, Nancy 2414 Sycamore Ln
Wallace, Dan Co Rd 2
Wallace, Donald 3517 Market
Wallace, Frank J St Rt 266
Wallace, Jack D Market St
Wallace, John School St
Wallace, Larry A 2311 E St Rt 266
Wallace, Ray B 2611 E River Rd SE
Wallace, Roger N St Rt 266
Wallace, Ron St Rt 266
Wallace, Steve Co Rd 60
Wallace, Tom 2401 Ervin Ln
Ward, Carl & Mary Co Rd 2

Weaver, Gary Co Rd 92
Weaver, Gerald 294 E St Rt 266 SE
Weaver, Gregory A Co Rd 92 Malta
Webb, "Foxy" Claude Jr 430 N Taylor
      Hollow Rd NE
Webb, Harold Co Rd 6
Webb, Ralph St Rt 376
Webb, Ted & Angie 6188 St Rt 792
Webb, Wilbert Tieber Rd
Wells, L Darlene 1920 Jackson
Wells, Jerry R Ti[e]ber Rd
West, Orville R Co Rd 2
Whipkey, Robert E St Rt 792
White, Connie L Co Rd 66
White, Craig Orr St Rt 266
White Donald D 2662 Co Rd 6 E
White, Glen Co Rd 6
White, Gerald Wash. Co Rd 18
White, Gerald L Palmer TR 18
White, Donald SR 266
White Ronald Co Rd 6
White, Thomas E Main St
White, Travis Twp Rd 23
Wilcoxin, Fama Palmer Twp Rd 6
Willgues, Alfred Co Rd 2
Williams, Lucy E Mrs Elmwood St
Wilson, Ted Lightner Rd
Winebrenner, William Sr St Rt 376
Winner, Russell RD 2
Winton, Mariwynne E Co Rd 36
Wood, David Michael 2750 E St Rt 266 SE
Work, Aaron 2606 E River Rd
Work, Harry L Wash. Cr Rd 18
Wright, R D Co Rd 2 Malta
Wyers, Dwight St Rt 676
Wylie, Glenn Rosewood St

Y

Young, Dennis E 6360 S Tabor Ridge Rd
Young, Camilla 2311 St. Rt 266
Young, John F Co Rd 36
Young, Otto B South St
Young, Willis Co Rd 36

Z

Zumbro, Daniel R Cleveland Av
Zumbro, Marian RD 3

Appendix J

U.S. Census of Population and Housing Stockport, Ohio

April 7-10, 1950

U.S. Department of Commerce Bureau of the Census

Cleo M. (*nee* Kirkbride) Morris
Enumerator

State: Ohio
County: Morgan
Incorporated Place: Stockport
E.D. Number: 58-23

Date: April 6, 1950
Enumerator: Cleo M. Morris
Checked by: Warren F. Parsons, April 7
Sheet Number: 1

Form P1 — 1950 Census of Population and Housing

Notes:
1) Traveling east - Right side of street
2) This man is known to be 10 years older than age given.

Line	Dwelling #	On farm?	Name	Relationship	Race	Sex	Age	Marital	Birthplace	Work last week	Looking	Kind of work	Industry	Class
1	1	no	Bachelor, Dayton C.	Head	W	M	39	Mar	Ohio	Wk		40	Pipe Fitting	River Gas Co	P
2			—, Eleanor	wife	W	F	41	Mar	Ohio	H	no no no		Housework	Home	NP
3			—, Gary R.	son	W	M	14	Nev	Ohio	ot	yes	8		Paper Rt	Publishing Co	P
4	2	no no	Rodgers, Hazel D.	Head	W	F	52	D	Ohio	H	no no no		Housework	Home	
5	3	no no	Lane, Stanley	Head	W	M	30	Mar	Ohio	Wk		60	Salesman	Retail Hardware	P
6			—, Eula C	wife	W	F	28	Mar	Ohio	H	no no no		Housework	Home	
7			—, James L	son	W	M	4	Nev	Ohio						
8			—, Joann L	dau	W	F	1	Nev	Ohio						
9	4		No one home. See sheet 73 line 17												
10	5		No one home. See sheet 71 line 1												
11	6	no no	Cheadle, Malcom B	Head	W	M	36	Mar	Ohio	Wk		60	Driving Truck	Strip coal Mine	O
12			—, Josephine L	wife	W	F	31	Mar	Ohio	H	no no no		Housework	Home	NP
13			—, Donna J	Dau	W	F	11	Nev	Ohio						
14			—, Mary A	Dau	W	F	8	Nev	Ohio						
15	7	no no	Boley, Chester R	Head	W	M	42	Mar	Ohio	Wk		60	Operating Machinery	Strip coal Mine	P
16			—, Mary L	wife	W	F	33	Mar	Ohio	H	no no no		Housework	Home	NP
17			—, Gary F	son	W	M	10	Nev	Ohio						
18			—, Larry G	son	W	M	7	Nev	Ohio						
19			—, Edward L	son	W	M	1	Nev	Ohio						
20	8	no no	Ring, Herman M	Head	W	M	58	Mar	Ohio	Wk		30	Carpenter Trade	Private Person	P
21			—, Eva M	wife	W	F	45	Mar	Ohio	H	no no no		Housework	Home	NP
22			—, Mildred G	Dau	W	F	18	Nev	Ohio	ot	yes	54	Baby Sitting	Private Home	P
23			—, H. Devere	son	W	M	14	Nev	Ohio	ot	no no no				
24	9	no no	Bishop, Clarence R	Head	W	M	62	Mar	Ohio	Wk		60	Manager	Retail Feed Store	P
25			—, Anna L	wife	W	F	57	Mar	Ohio	H	no no no		Housewife	Home	NP
26	10	no no	Adrian, Laura	Head	W	F	77	Wd	Ohio	H	no no no		Housewife	Home	NP
27	11	no no	McHugh, Thomas J	Head	W	M	73	Mar	Ohio	Wk		36	Carrying Mail	U.S. Post Office	P
28			McHugh, Mary A	wife	W	F	67	Mar	Ohio	H	no no no		Housewife	Home	NP
29	12		No one home - See Sheet 71 line 3												
30	13	no no	White, James C	Head	W	M	26	Mar	Ohio	Wk		40	Helper Boiler Rep	Am Power Co	P

1950 CENSUS OF POPULATION AND HOUSING

State: Ohio
County: Morgan
Incorporated Place or Township: Rockport
E.D. Number: 58-23
Date: April 7, 1950
Enumerator: Cleo M. Morris
Sheet Number: 2

Line	Serial #	Name	Relationship	Race	Sex	Age	Marital Status	Birthplace	Working?	Hours	Occupation	Industry	Class
1		White, Betty L.	Wife	W	F	23	Mar	Tenn.	H, no				
2		—, Patricia J.	Dau	W	F	5	Nev	California					
3		—, Barbara J.	Dau	W	F	Apr	Nev	Ohio					
4	14	no one home. See page 71 - line 6											
5	15	No one home. See Page 72 line 20											
6	16 - no no	Weaver, Laura L.	Head	W	F	52	Wd	Ohio	H, no no no				
7	17 - no no	Cain, Joseph L.	Head	W	M	37	Mar	Ohio	Wk	60	Operates truck	Retail Hardware	P 683 686
8		—, Vera L.	Wife	W	F	32	Mar	Ohio	H, no no no				
9		—, Joseph R.	Son	W	M	5	Nev	Ohio					
10		—, Carlos C.	Son	W	M	4	Nev	Ohio					
11		—, Mildred C.	Dau	W	F	3	Oct Nev	Ohio					
12	18 - no no	Burfield, Robert L.	Head	W	M	22	Mar	Ohio	Wk	50	Assembly Line	Plow Co.	P 603 561
13		—, Wanda E.	Wife	W	F	20	Mar	Ohio	H, no no no				
14		—, Jane E.	Dau	W	F	1	Nev	Ohio					
15	19 - no no	McMorrow, Ernest C.	Head	W	M	39	Mar	W.Va	Wk	49	Assembly Line	Plow Co.	P 470 356
16		—, Nellie P.	Wife	W	F	33	Mar	W.Va	Wk	59	Proper	Retail 10¢ Store	O 240 647
17		—, Robert C.	Son	W	M	4	Nev	W.Va					
18		Weaver, Cynthia J.	Lodger	W	F	2	Nev	Ohio					
19	20 no no	Calendine, Jarold L.	Head	W	M	24	Mar	Ohio	Wk	60	Mechanic	Garage	O 550 816
20		—, Neva B.	Wife	W	F	23	Mar	Ohio	H, no no no				
21		—, Linda D.	Dau	W	F	1	Nev	Ohio					
22	21 no no	Calendine, Billy A.	Head	W	M	29	Mar	Ohio	Wk	40	Postal work	U.S. Post Office	G 310 1062
23		—, Mildred N.	Wife	W	F	29	Mar	Ohio	H, no no no				
24		—, Roger H.	Son	W	M	3	Nev	Ohio					
25		—, Karen L.	Dau	W	F	2	Nev	Ohio					
26		—, Richard A.	Son	W	M	1	Nev	Ohio					
27	22 no no	Van Fossen, David S.	Head	W	M	42	Mar	Ohio	Wk	20	Cabinet work	own Shop	O 565 6783
28		—, Margaret L.	Wife	W	F	42	Mar	Ohio	Wk, no no no	40	Agriculture Teacher	Senior High	G 75 858
29		Appler, Raymond	Lodger	W	M	27	Nev	Ohio	Wk	40	Mechanic	Garage	P 550 816
30	23	no one home. See sheet 71 line 14											

1950 CENSUS OF POPULATION AND HOUSING

State: Ohio
County: Morgan
Incorporated Place or Township: Stockport
E.D. Number: 58-23
Date: April 7
Sheet Number: 3
Enumerator: Cleo M. Morris

Notes: Commencing west on Main Street - Left side of street.

Line	House #	Name	Relationship	Race	Sex	Age	Marital	Birthplace	Employment	Hours	Occupation	Industry	Class
1	24	No one home See Page 72 Line 9											
2	25	Harkins, James O.	Head	W	M	39	mar	Ohio	wk	65	Prop	Retail Grocery	O
3		—, Frances J.	Wife	W	F	33	mar	Ohio	wk	30	Science Teacher	Senior High	
4		—, Betty E.	Dau	W	F	7	nev	Ohio					
5		—, Jean L.	Dau	W	F	3	nev	Ohio					
6	26	Not home See Sheet 71 Line 27											
7	27	Not home See Sheet 73 Line 9											
8	28	Brookover, Reed	Head	W	M	59	mar	Ohio	ot		no no no		
9		—, Ruby	Wife	W	F	56	mar	W.Va.	H		no no no		
10		—, Kenneth R.	Son	W	M	17	nev	Ohio	ot		no no no		
11		—, Rawleigh L.	Son	W	M	26	nev	Ohio	wk	40	Clerk (Billing)	N-W Railroad	P
12	29	No one home See Sheet 74 Line 6											
13	30	No one home See Sheet 74 Line 9											
14	31	No one home See Sheet 71 Line 17											
15	32	Fulmer, Earl R.	Head	W	M	30	mar	Ohio	wk	48	Proprietor	Garage	O
16		—, Mary L.	Wife	W	F	25	mar	Ohio	H		no no no		
17		—, Sharon S.	Dau	W	F	1	nev	Ohio					
18	33	Addis, W. Otto	Head	W	M	62	mar	Ohio	U		no no yes 40	Housework	Hotel	O
19		—, Clara B.	Wife	W	F	57	mar	Ohio	H		no no no		
20		—, Chester B.	Son	W	M	39	nev	Ohio	wk	48	Truck Driver	Ohio Power Co	P
21		—, John Jr.	Son	W	M	22	nev	Ohio	wk		Saw work	Sash and Door	P
22		—, Carl D.	Son	W	M	22	nev	Ohio	wk	40	Saw work	Sash & Door	P
23		Davis, Dana	Lodger	W	M	75	wd	Ohio	U				
24		Coen, James N.	Lodger	W	M	85	wd	Ohio	U				
25		Blunden, Eva	Lodger	W	F	84	wd	Ohio	U				
26		Wootton, William E.	Head	W	M	77	nev	Ohio	wk	64	Salesman (Prop)	Retail Grocery	O
27		—, Leslie H.	Brother	W	M	67	mar	Ohio	wk	64	Salesman	Retail Grocery	P
28		McDonald, Minnie N.	Sister	W	F	81	wd	Ohio	H		no no no		
29		Wootton, Alta F.	Sister-in-law	W	F	60	mar	Ohio	H		no no no		
30	35	Faires, Harry D.	Head	W	M	67	wd	Ohio	wk	65	Prop.	Retail Grocery	O

1950 CENSUS OF POPULATION AND HOUSING

State: Ohio
County: Morgan
Incorporated Place or Township: Stockport
E.D. Number: 58-23
Date Sheet Started: April 7, 1950
Enumerator's Signature: Elis M. Morris
Sheet Number: 4

Note: "This man gets aged pension but said he couldn't keep account because of lack of education."

Line	House #	Household #	Name	Relationship	Race	Sex	Age	Marital	Birthplace	Working?	Hours	Occupation	Industry	Class
1			Faires, Helen B.	Dau.	W	F	30	Nev.	Ohio	wk.	30	Primary teacher	School teacher	
2	36	no no	Faires, Frank R.	Head	W	M	33	Mar.	Ohio	wk.	62	Salesman	Retail Grocery	O
3			—, Mary R.	Wife	W	F	30	Mar.	Penna.	H.	no no no			
4			—, E. Lucille	Dau.	W	F	1	Nev.	Ohio					
5			—, Rebecca L.	Dau.	W	F	Sep.	Nev.	Ohio					
6	37	no no	Hayes, Wm. J.	Head	W	M	28	Mar.	Ohio	wk.	48	Production Clerk	Pling Manufacturing Co.	P
7			—, Alice K.	Wife	W	F	26	Mar.	Ohio	H.	no no no			
8			—, Carol A.	Dau.	W	F	Nov.	Nev.	Ohio					
9			—, Diana S.	Dau.	W	F	Nov.	Nev.	Ohio					
10	38	no no	Newsom, Don M.	Head	W	M	30	Mar.	Ohio	wk.	67	Operates Duster	Wholesale Plow Co.	P
11			—, Ethel L.	Wife	W	F	25	Mar.	Ohio	H.	no no no			
12			—, Marion E.	Son	W	M	3	Nev.	Ohio					
13	39		No one home See sheet 73 Line 21											
14	40	no no	Linn, Wilson	Head	W	M	81	Wd.	Ohio	H.	no no			
15	41		No one home See sheet 71 line 13											
16	42	no no	Wallace, W. Loyd	Head	W	M	52	Mar.	Ohio	H.	no no			
17			—, Nellie M.	Wife	W	F	61	Mar.	Ohio					
18	43		Vacant House											
19	44	no no	Calendine, Leonard H.	Head	W	M	56	Mar.	Ohio	wk.	60	Prop.	Retail Hdw.	O
20			—, Lottie	Wife	W	F	56	Mar.	Ohio	wk.	35	Bookkeeper	Retail Hdw.	NP
21			—, Janet	Dau.	W	F	8	Nev.	Ohio					
22	45	no no	Calendine, Landon L.	Head	W	M	37	Mar.	Ohio	wk.	49	Shipping Clerk	Wholesale Groc.	P
23			—, Belva C.	Wife	W	F	31	Mar.	Ohio	H.	no no no			
24			—, Robert L.	Son	W	M	14	Nev.	Ohio	at	no no no			
25			—, Delores J.	Dau.	W	F	13	Nev.	Ohio					
26			—, J. Kay	Dau.	W	F	6	Nev.	Ohio					
27	46		No one home See sheet 71 line 10											
28	47		No one home See sheet 73 Line 29											
29	48	no no	Rardin, Clint C.	Head	W	M	70	D	Ohio	U				
30	49	no no	Fisher, Cora	Head	W	F	80	Wd.	Ohio	U				

1950 Census of Population and Housing

State: Ohio
County: Morgan
Incorporated place or township: Stockport
E.D. Number: 58-23
Date: April 8, 1950
Enumerator: Ches Morris
Sheet Number: 5

Line	HH#	Name	Relation	Race	Sex	Age	Marital	Birthplace	Work	Hours	Occupation	Industry
1	50	Williams, Clarence R	Head	W	M	50	Mar	Ohio	Wk	40	Bridge Tender	Gov't Engineers
2		—, Wilma L	Wife	W	F	47	Mar	Ohio	H			
3		—, Nelda C	Dau	W	F	16	Nev	Ohio	Wk	6	Ticket Seller	Port Theater
4	51	No one home See Sheet 73 Line 12										
5	52	Mercer, Harley E	Head	W	M	58	Mar	Ohio	Wk			
6		—, Bessie M	Wife	W	F	58	Mar	Ohio	H	6	Postal Clerk	U.S. Post Office
7	53	No one home See Sheet 73 Line 15										
8	54	Powelson, Ellen E	Head	W	F	70	Wd	Ohio	Wk	40	English-Latin	Senior High
9	55	Ellis, Mary A	Head	W	F	75	Wd	Ohio	H			
10	56	Lowther, Boyd D	Head	W	M	29	Mar	W. Va	Wk	48	Feed grinder and	Retail Feed Store
11		—, Mary L	Wife	W	F	22	Mar	Ohio	H			
12		—, Michael D	Son	W	M	2	Nev	Ohio				
13	57	Vacant House										
14	58	No one home See page 71 line 24										
15	59	Sells, C. Blaine	Head	W	M	43	Mar	Ohio	Wk	30	Primary Teach	County Grade School
16		—, Mary E	Wife	W	F	29	Mar	Ohio	H			
17		—, Dovyleene D	Dau	W	F	10	Nev	Ohio				
18		—, Terry	Son	W	M	8	Nev	Ohio				
19	60	No one home – See page 71 line 22										
20	61	Brannan, Roxanne	Head	W	F	73	Wd	Ohio	H			
21		Benjamin, Jay F	Grandson	W	M	8	Nev	Ohio				
22	62	Bailey, George A	Head	W	M	79	Mar	Ohio	U			
23		—, Effie L	Wife	W	F	69	Mar	Ohio	H			
24		Robey, Wm	Lodger	W	M	33	Div	Ohio	Wk	40	Repair Crew	Railroad
25		Fleming, Ernest L	Lodger	W	M	79	Wd	Ohio	Wk	36	Farm work	Farm
26	63	Bachelor, K. Yode	Head	W	M	39	Mar	Ohio	Wk	48	Wood work	Lumber Mill
27		—, Katherine L	Wife	W	F	34	Mar	Ohio	H			
28		—, W. Kenneth	Son	W	M	10	Nev	Ohio				
29	64	McCoy, Kenneth A	Head	W	M	36	Mar	Ohio	Wk	40	Postal Clerk	U.S. Post Office
30		—, Norma R	Wife	W	F	28	Mar	Ohio	H			

1950 CENSUS OF POPULATION AND HOUSING

State: Ohio
County: Morgan
Incorporated place or township: Stockport
E.D. Number: 58-23
Enumerator: Clea M. Morris
Checked by: Warren F. Parsons, April 11
Sheet Number: 6

Line	House #	Farm?	Name	Relationship	Race	Sex	Age	Marital	State of Birth	Work last week?	Looking for work?	Hours worked	Occupation	Industry	Class of worker
1			McCoy, Jane A.	Dau	W	F	1	Nev	Ohio						
2	65		No one home See Page 73 Line 23												
3	66 - no		McMillan, Earl W.	Head	W	M	39	Mar	Ark.	ot	no	yes yes	Cuts Timber	Sawmill	P 6743071
4			—, Iva	Wife	W	F	35	Mar	Ark.	H	no	no no			
5			—, Wanda S.	Dau	W	F	13	Nev	Ark.						
6			—, Billy E.	Son	W	M	8	Nev	Ark.						
7			—, Patsy L.	Dau	W	F	7	Nev	Ark.						
8			—, Janice M.	Dau	W	F	5	Nev	Ark.						
9	67		No one home See Page 72 line 14												
10	68		No one home See Page 72 line 2												
11	69 - no	no	Wallace, Quitera	Head	W	F	75	Wd	Ohio	U.					
12			—, Almagro W.	Bro.	W	M	78	Nev	Ohio	ot	no	no no			
13	70		No one home See page 71 line 26												
14	71 - no	no	Brittigan, Bertha C.	Head	W	F	68	Wd	Ohio	H	no	no no			
15	72 yes	1	No one home see Page 71 line 20												
16	73 - no	no	Bole, Jesse H.	Head	W	M	65	Mar	Ohio	t	ons	yes no	Teamster	Hauling Lumber	P 9605263
17			—, Ola	Wife	W	F	65	Mar	Ohio	U.		yes			
18	74 - no	no	Calvin, Cecil L.	Head	W	M	23	Mar	Ohio	U.					
19			—, Margaret M.	Wife	W	F	20	Mar	Ohio	H	no	no no			
20			—, Cecilia C.	Dau	W	F	2	Nev	Ohio						
21	75 - no	no	Teeters, John R.	Head	W	M	59	Mar	Penna	H	no	no no			
22			—, Bessie W.	Wife	W	F	57	Mar	Calif.	H	no	no no			
23	76 - no	no	Carr, Orzen J.	Head	W	M	63	Mar	Ohio	H	no	no no			
24			—, Ion	Wife	W	F	63	Mar	Ohio	H	no	no no			
25	77 - no	no	Rowland, Delbert O.	Head	W	M	45	Mar	Ohio	H					
26			—, Mabel M.	Wife	W	F	45	Mar	Ohio	H	no	no no			
27			—, Wayne E.	Son	W	M	15	Nev	Ohio	H	no	no no			
28			—, Paul E.	Son	W	M	12	Nev	Ohio						
29			—, Alice L.	Dau	W	F	11	Nev	Ohio						
30	78 - no	no	Fleming, Harry C.	Head	W	M	42	Mar	Ohio	Wk		54	Labor	Gravel Pit	P 650236

1950 CENSUS OF POPULATION AND HOUSING

State: Ohio
County: Morgan
Incorporated place or township: Stockport
E.D. Number: 58-23
Date sheet started: April 12, 1950
Enumerator's signature: Chas M Morris
Sheet Number: 9

Line	Serial	Name	Relationship	Race	Sex	Age	Marital	Birthplace	Work status	Hours	Occupation	Industry	Class
1		Harkins, Anna Mae	wife	W	F	27	mar	Ohio	H	no no no			
2		—, Wm H. Jr.	Son	W	M	3	nev	Ohio					
3		—, Carlene S.	Dau	W	F	2	nev	Ohio					
4	105 no yes 4	Evans, Glenn J.	Head	W	M	49	mar	Ohio	Ot	no no yes	Rural Mail Carrier	U.S. Post Office	F 335.9062
5		—, Catharine C.	wife	W	F	45	mar	Ohio	H	no no no			
6		—, Martha L.	Dau	W	F	17	nev	Ohio	Ot	no no no			
7		—, Janet E.	Dau	W	F	14	nev	Ohio	Ot	no no no			
8	106	Vacant House											
9	107	No one Home See Sheet 74 Line 2											
10	108 no no	Pierpoint, Lindley E.	Head	W	M	56	mar	Ohio	Wk	20	Carpenter Work	Private Home	O 515.246 3
11		—, Ruby C.	wife	W	F	57	mar	Ohio	H	no no no			
12	109	Vacant House											
13	110	No one home See page 72 line 5											
14	111	No one home See Page 74 Line 11											
15	112 no no	Walker, Earl E.	Head	W	M	37	mar	Ohio	Wk	15	Wiring Houses	Electrical Work	O 515.246 3
16		—, Grace L.	wife	W	F	37	mar	Ohio	H	no no no			
17		—, Marian J.	Dau	W	F	16	nev	Ohio	Ot	no no no			
18		—, Kilburn E.	Son	W	M	13	nev	Ohio					
19		—, R. Keith	Son	W	M	7	nev	Ohio					
20		—, Richard L.	Son	W	M	1	nev	Ohio					
21	113	No one home See Sheet 74 Line 4											
22	114 no no	Rollison, Fred	Head	W	M	52	mar	Ohio	Wk	70	Prop. Filling	Retail Gasoline Station	O 221.665
23		—, Allie M.	wife	W	F	51	mar	Ohio	U				
24	115	Vacant House											
25	116 no no	Hoover, Dayton	Head	W	M	50	mar	Ohio	Wk	44	Labor	Wholesale Flour Co	P 970.626 1
26		—, Thanya E.	wife	W	F	45	mar	Ohio	H	no no no			
27		—, Richard W.	Son	W	M	19	nev	Ohio	Wk	40	Making Cement Blk	Cement Block Co	P 970.317 1
28		—, Vonda L.	Dau	W	F	17	nev	Ohio	Ot yes	18	sales girl	retail grocery	P 411.661
29	117 no no	Geddes, Riley P.	Head	W	M	69	nev	Ohio	U				
30	118 no no	Wallace, Edgar D.	Head	W	M	62	mar	Ohio	Wk	5	Drilling	contract water well drilling	P 970.246 3

1950 CENSUS OF POPULATION AND HOUSING

State: Ohio
County: Morgan
Incorporated Place or Township: Stockport
E.D. Number: 58-23
Sheet Number: 8
Date: April 10, 1950
Enumerator: Cleo M. Morris
Checked by: Warren F. Parsons, April 11, 1950

Line	Serial no.	House no.	Name	Relationship	Race	Sex	Age	Marital	Birthplace	Working?	Hours	Occupation	Industry	Class
1			Barfield, Ina L	Wife	W	F	60	mar	Ohio		no no no			
2			—, Carl C	Son	W	M	24	mar	Ohio	Wk	27	Carpenter work	Wholesale Floor Co	P 510026
3			—, Ray S	Son	W	M	29	mar	Ohio	Wk	40	Labor	Wholesale Floor Co	P 970626
4			—, Alma E	Dau-in-law	W	F	27	mar	Florida	H	no no no			
5			—, Larry L	Grandson	W	M	3	nev	Ohio					
6			—, David A	Grandson	W	M	2	nev	Ohio					
7			—, Barbara C	Grand Dau	W	F	June nev	Alabama						
8			—, Sue N Still	Grand Dau	W	F	7	nev	Ohio					
9	96-no no		McCoy, Thomas H	Head	W	M	70	mar	Ohio	U				
10			—, Ida A	Wife	W	F	58	mar	Ohio	H	no no no			
11	97-no no		Cowger, Otto	Head	W	M	74	mar	Kansas	Wk	18	Barber Work	Barber Shop	O 7408493
12			—, Anna	Wife	W	F	82	mar	Ohio	U				
13	98-no no		Bobey, Charles K	Head	W	M	26	mar	Ohio	Wk	40	Section	Railroad	P 9705001
14			—, Melba A	Wife	W	F	25	mar	Ohio	H	no no no			
15			—, Sandra S	Dau	3	W	F	3	nev	Ohio				
16			—, Betty L	Dau	3	W	F	Jan nev	Ohio					
17	99		No one home See Sheet 73 line 4											
18	100-no yes 3		Lingfellow, George F	Head	W	M	62	mar	Ohio	Wk	16	Timber-Farming	Farm	O 820051
19			—, Savilla C	Wife	W	F	56	mar	Ohio	H	no no no			
20	101-no no		Morris, Dale L	Head	W	M	34	mar	Ohio	Wk	54	Operate Dragline	Gravel Co	P 522361
21			—, Cleo M	Wife	W	F	33	mar	Ohio	Wk	20	Enumerator Census	Bureau of Census	590716
22			—, Shirley E	Dau	W	F	15	nev	Ohio	ot				
23			—, Virginia J	Dau	W	F	10	nev	Ohio					
24	102-no no		Kern, Weir	Head	W	M	39	mar	Penna	Wk	54	Operate Dragline	Gravel Co	P 522261
25			—, Mary Lou	Wife	W	F	30	mar	Ohio	H	no no no			
26			—, Richard L	Son	W	M	12	nev	Ohio					
27			—, Madelon A	Dau	W	F	10	nev	Ohio					
28	103-no no		Douth, Benj Elton	Head	W	M	72	mar	Ohio	U				
29			—, Jessie L	Wife	W	F	75	mar	Ohio	H	no no no			
30	104-no no		Harkins, Wm Russell	Head	W	M	28	mar	Ohio	Wk	35	Commercial Teacher	County Senior High	G 012802

1950 CENSUS OF POPULATION AND HOUSING

State: Ohio
County: Morgan
Incorporated Place or Township: Stockport
E.D. Number: 58-23
Date Sheet Started: April 10, 1950
Enumerator's Signature: Clea M. Morris
Checked by: Warren F. Parsons on April 11, 1950
Sheet Number: 7

Line	House #	Serial #	Is this house on a place of 3 or more acres?	Name (Last name first)	Relationship	Race	Sex	Age	Marital status	State or country of birth	Naturalized	Working?	Looking for work?	Has job?	Hours worked	Occupation	Industry	Class of worker
1		no	no	Fleming, Dolores	Wife	W	F	32	Mar	Mich.		H	no	no				
2	79	no	no	White, Mary C.	Head	W	F	80	Wd	Ohio		H	no	no				
3	80			No one home See Page 72 line 12														
4	81	no	no	Durbin, Robt A.	Head	W	M	49	Mar	Ohio		wk			56	Post Master	U S Post Office	P 2709061
5				—, Margaret D.	Wife	W	F	47	Mar	Ohio		wk			30	Postal Clerk	U S Post Office	P 3904941
6	82			No one home See Page 73 Line 9														
7	83			See Page 72 line 7 (No one home)														
8	84			No one home See Page 72 line 19														
9	85	no	no	Colerick, Frank D.	Head	W	M	64	Mar	Ohio		wk			12	Carpenter	Own Business	O 5102463
10				—, Myrtie D.	Wife	W	F	74	Mar	Ohio		H	no	no				
11	86	no	no	Brokaw, Wm	Head	W	M	32	Mar	Ohio		wk			40	Saw Mill	Own Business	O 6903073
12				—, Evelyn L.	Wife	W	F	28	Mar	Ky.		H	no	no				
13				—, Jo Ann	Dau	W	F	2	Nev	Ohio								
14				—, Donald L.	Son	W	M	04/14	Nev	Ohio								
15	87	no	no	Calendine, Zetta G.	Head	W	F	73	Wd	Ohio		H	no	no				
16				Darnell, Mary E.	Sister	W	F	75	Wd	Ohio		H	no	no				
17	88	no	no	Geddes, Murray T.	Head	W	M	74	Mar	Ohio		wk			24	Painting		O 5642463
18				—, Mildred A.	Wife	W	F	52	Mar	Ohio		H	no	no				
19	89	no	no	James, Fred E.	Head	W	M	56	Mar	Ohio		wk			18	Produce Buyer	Wholesale Prod.	O
20				—, Wilda E.	Wife	W	F	49	Mar	Ohio		H	no	no				
21				—, Jeannene	Dau.	W	F	15	Nev	Ohio		at	no	no				
22	90			No one home See page 72 line 1														
23	91	no	no	Green, Sandford W.	Head	W	M	75	Nev	Ohio		H	no	no				
24	92	yes	2	Simpson, Blanche M.	Head	W	F	71	Wd	Ohio		H	no	no				
25				Newton, Mary J.	Dau	W	F	44	Mar	Ohio		wk			40	Primary Teacher	Country Grade School	
26				Henry, Emma	Sister-in-Law	W	F	79	Wd	Ohio		H	no	no				
27	93	no	no	Hooper, Ida L.	Head	W	F	71	Wd	Ohio		H	no	no				
28	94	no	no	Boles, Charley F.	Head	W	M	69	Mar	Ohio		at	no	yes		Haul lumber	Barretts Stave Company	O
29				—, Josie M.	Wife	W	F	70	Mar	Ohio		H	no	no				
30	95	no	no	Burfield, Selby C.	Head	W	M	64	Mar	Ohio		U						

1950 CENSUS OF POPULATION AND HOUSING

State: Ohio
County: Morgan
Incorporated place or township: (no report)
E.D. Number: 58-23
Date sheet started: April 12
Enumerator: Cleo M Morris
Sheet number: 10

Line	House #	Name	Relationship	Race	Sex	Age	Marital	Birthplace	Working?	Hours	Occupation	Industry	Code
1		Wallace, Tillie	wife	W	F	58	Mar	Ohio	H				
2	119 – no no	Nott, Eva	Head	W	F	72	Wid	Ohio	H	no no			
3		—, Berlyn	Son	W	M	43	Nev	Ohio	wk		12 Installing Sink	Private Home	690-243
4	120 – no no	Henry, Myrtle L	Head	W	F	72	Wid	Ohio	H	no no			
5	121 – no no	McCoy, Harry B	Head	W	M	34	Mar	Ohio	wk		40 Driving Truck	Transport	683-526
6		—, Laura D	wife	W	F	34	Mar	Ohio	H	no no			
7		—, Ellen M	Dau	W	F	7	Nev	Ohio					
8		—, Carole D	Dau	W	F	5	Nev	Ohio					
9	122	No one home See Page		72 line 3									
10	123	no one home See Page		74 line 1									
11	124	no one home See Sheet		73 line 1									
12	125 – no no	Wallace, Friend E	Head	W	M	48	Mar	Ohio	wk		54 Shovel Operator	Strip Mine	650-216
13		—, Dorothy O	wife	W	F	37	Mar	Ohio	H	no no no			
14		—, Denny O	Son	W	M	15	Div		at yes		4 Farm Helper	Farm	820-105
15		—, MaryAnna	Dau	W	F	3	Nev	Ohio					
16		—, James E	Son	W	M	2	Nev	Ohio					
17		—, Sara D	Dau	W	F	mar	Nev	Ohio					
18	126 – no no	Wells, Wilbert	Head	W	M	32	Mar	Ky	wk		35 Driving Truck	Dairy	632-627
19		—, Rosemary E	wife	W	F	29	Mar	Ohio		no no no			
20		—, Barbara A	Dau	W	F	7	Nev	Ohio					
21		—, Wayne	Father	W	M	79	Wid	W Va	H				
22	127 – no no	Campbell, Harvey J	Head	W	M	67	Mar	W Va	H				
23		—, Ora L	wife	W	F	61	Mar	Ohio	H				
24		—, Herbert J	Son	W	M	30	Sep	Ohio	wk		50 Steel Cutter	Wholesale Prod Co	690-436
25		Harris, Audrey J	Dau	W	F	38	Sep	Ohio	H	no no no			
26		—, Cheryl L	Grand dau	W	F	12	Nev	Ohio					
27		—, Thomas	Grandson	W	M	10	Nev	Ohio					
28		—, Edward	Grandson	W	M	8	Nev	Ohio					
29		—, Charles J	Grandson	W	M	7	Nev	Ohio					
30		—, Wm L	Grandson	W	M	4	Nev	Ohio					

1950 CENSUS OF POPULATION AND HOUSING

State: Ohio
County: Morgan
Incorporated Place or Township: Stockport
E.D. Number: 58-23
Date Sheet Started: April 12, 1950
Enumerator's Signature: Cleo M. Morris
Checked by: Warren F. Parsons, April 17, 1950
Sheet Number: 11

Line	Serial No.	Is house on farm?	3+ acres?	Name	Relationship	Race	Sex	Age	Marital	Birthplace	Working?	Hours	Occupation	Industry	Class
1				Harris, Gerald Dean	Grandson	W	M	Sept. New		Ohio					
2	128—no	no		Van Fossen, Donald A.	Head	W	M	42	mar	Ohio	Wk	50	Embalming	Funeral Director	P 0548441
3				—, Marjorie N.	Wife	W	F	43	mar	Ohio	H	no no no			
4				—, Malaia J.	Dau	W	F	6	New	Ohio					
5	129—no	no		McDermott, Edward	Head	W	M	73	mar	Ohio	U				
6				—, Mary H.	Wife	W	F	69	mar	Ohio	H	no no no			
7	130—no	no		Martin, Ida M.	Head	W	F	72	wd	Ohio	H				
8				Metcalfe, Nona	Sister	W	F	78	wd	Ohio	Wk	112	Telephone	Upstairs	210 5781
9	131—no	no		Mosier, Harold J.	Head	W	M	47	mar	Ohio	Wk	90	Mechanic	Auto Repair Garage	O 550 8163
10				—, Vesta C.	Wife	W	F	45	mar	Ohio	H	no no no			
11	132			No one home See Sheet 72 line 21											
12	133—no	no		Keffer, Leroy	Head	W	M	29	mar	W.Va.	Wk	44	Feed Salesman	Retail Feed Store	P 4906181
13				—, Martha	Wife	W	F	24	mar	Georgia	H	no no no			
14				—, Ronald L.	Son	W	M	3	New	Ohio					
15				—, Gary L.	Son	W	M	1	New	Georgia					
16	134			No one home See sheet 72 line 22											
17	135—no	yes	5	Cross, Harry	Head	W	M	73	mar	Ohio	Ot	no no no			
18				—, Mary	Wife	W	F	70	mar	W.Va.	H	no no no			
19	136—no	no		Ferrebee, James R.	Head	W	M	30	mar	W.Va.	Ot	no yes	Operates Bulldozer	Pipe Line Construction	P 512 2431
20				—, Eileen B.	Wife	W	F	30	mar	Ohio	H	no no no			
21				—, Barbara L.	Dau	W	F	11	New	Ohio					
22				—, Linda S.	Dau	W	F	2	New	Ohio					
23	137			Vacant											
24	138			Vacant											
25	139			Vacant											
26	140—no	yes	6	No one home See Sheet 73 line 10											
27	141—yes		6	Schaad, John F.	Head	W	M	30	mar	Ohio	Wk	60	Farm work	Farm	O 10 1 5 3
28				—, Margaret R.	Wife	W	F	27	mar	Ohio	H	no no no			4106 1
29				—, John Paul	Son	W	M	June New		Ohio					
30				—, Carl Jr.	Bro	W	M	24	mar	Ohio	Wk	60	Farm work	Farm	O 10 1 5 3

1950 CENSUS OF POPULATION AND HOUSING

State: Ohio
County: Morgan
Incorporated Place or Township: Stockport
E.D. Number: 58-23
Date: April 13, 1950
Enumerator: Cleo M. Morris
Sheet Number: 12

Line	House #	Name	Relationship	Race	Sex	Age	Marital	Birthplace	Employment	Hours	Occupation	Industry
1		Schaad, Dorothy A.	Sister-in-law	W	F	24	Mar	Ohio	H			
2		—, Christopher L.	Nephew	W	M	Dec	Nev	Ohio				
3	142	Locke, James L.	Head	W	M	37	Mar	W.Va.	ot			
4		—, Pauline O.	Wife	W	F	34	Mar	Ohio	H			
5		—, Virginia L.	Dau.	W	F	9	Nev	Ohio				
6		—, James F.	Son	W	M	7	Nev	Ohio				
7	143	Matthews, Wayne T.	Head	W	M	42	Mar	Ohio	wk	45	Supt.	Senior High
8		—, Ethel J.	Wife	W	F	24	Mar	Ohio	H			
9		—, Martha J.	Dau.	W	F	3	Nev	Ohio				
10	144	No one home — See Sheet 73 Line 24										
11	145	Pugh, Don W.	Head	W	M	31	Mar	Ohio	wk	30	Labor Farmer	Farm
12		—, Hazel V.	Wife	W	F	33	Mar	Ohio	H			
13		—, Christine	Dau.	W	F	8	Nev	Ohio				
14		—, Linda D.	Dau.	W	F	6	Nev	Ohio				
15		—, Brenda K.	Dau.	W	F	5	Nev	Ohio				
16		—, Wanda J.	Dau.	W	F	2	Nev	Ohio				
17	146	Thompson, Lillian	Head	W	F	82	Nev	Ohio	wk	30	Minister	Methodist Church
18	147	Cecil, Charles P.	Head	W	M	60	Mar	Va.	U			
19		—, Jetta L.	Wife	W	F	55	Mar	Ky.	H			
20		—, Wm. J.	Son	W	M	18	Nev	Ky.	ot			
21	148	Newberry, Chester M.	Head	W	M	69	Mar	Ohio	U			
22		—, Anna D.	Wife	W	F	65	Mar	Ohio	H			
23	149	Medley, Jason R.	Head	W	M	78	Mar	Ohio	ot			
24		—, Rose E.	Wife	W	F	75	Mar	Ohio	H			
25	150	Blind, Alva D.	Head	W	M	62	Mar	Ohio	U			
26		—, Stata O.	Wife	W	F	59	Mar	Ohio	H			
27	151	Blind, John L.	Head	W	M	65	Mar	Ohio	wk	72	Garden Work	Home
28		—, Mary N.	Wife	W	F	48	Mar	Ohio	H			
29		—, Merlyn G.	Son	W	M	15	Nev	Ill.	ot			

- 144 -

1950 Census of Population and Housing

State: Ohio
County: Morgan
Incorporated place or township: Stockport
E.D. Number: 58-23
Sheet Number: 71

Line	Address	Serial	House	Name (Last name first)	Relationship	Race	Sex	Age	Marital	Birthplace	Work?	Hours	Occupation	Industry	Class
1	West end Main	5	no no	Rowland, Lee D	Head	W	M	22	mar	Ohio	Wk	26	Welder	Ohio Power Co	P
2				—, Faye	Wife	W	F	18	mar	Ohio	H	no no no			
3	Across Church	12	no no	Locke, Russell B	Head	W	M	42	mar	W.Va.	U				
4				—, Mae	Wife	W	F	37	mar	Ohio	H	no no no			
5				—, Ray C	Son	W	M	13	nev	Ohio	Wk	40	S		
6		14	no no	Shaner, James W	Head	W	M	29	mar	Ohio	Wk	40	Spray Painting	Brown Equip Mfg Co	P
7				—, Captola ?	Wife	W	F	29	mar	Ohio	H	no no no			
8				—, Virginia L	Dau	W	F	3	nev	Ohio					
9				—, James M	Son	W	M	Apr	nev	Ohio					
10		46	no no	Coar, George W	Head	W	M	53	mar	Ohio	Wk	58	Janitor	High School	G
11				—, Sylvia J	Wife	W	F	45	mar	Ohio	H	no no no			
12				—, James A	Son	W	M	24	mar	Ohio	Wk	56	Lumber ?	Retail Lumber	P
13		41	no no	Patterson, Blanche	Head	W	F	66	wd	Ohio	H	no no no			
14		23	no no	Weaver, Eldon J	Head	W	M	21	mar	Ohio	Wk	54	Barber	Barber Shop	P
15			no no	—, Catharine D	Wife	W	F	19	mar	Ohio	H	no no no			
16				—, James S	Son	W	M	June	nev	Ohio					
17		31	no no	Ormiston, Vance B	Head	W	M	25	mar	Ohio	Wk	48	Labor	Ohio Power	P
18				—, F. Cleo	Wife	W	F	21	mar	Ohio	Wk	40	Waitress	Restaurant	P
19				Hindman, Jean	Lodger	W	F	20	nev	Ohio	Wk	32	Beautician	Beauty Parlor	O
20		72	no yes 1	Henry, Harry A	Head	W	M	73	mar	Ohio	Wk	60	Prop	Filling Station	O
21				—, Maggie M	Wife	W	F	72	mar	Ohio	H	no no no			
22		60	no no	Newton, Walter D	Head	W	M	70	wd	Ohio	U				
23				Welsh, Mary C	Sister	W	F	66	wd	Ohio	H	no no no			
24		58	no no	Newman, James S	Head	W	M	69	mar	Ohio	Wk	30	Paper Hanger	Own Business	O
25				—, Tresa B	Wife	W	F	64	mar	Ohio	H	no no no			
26		70	no no	Coleman, John	Head	W	M	78	wd	Ohio	U				
27		26	no no	James, Robt J	Head	W	M	74	wd	Ohio	S	10	Poultry Buyer	Poultry Business	P
28			no no	Barker, Charity A	Head	W	F	81	wd	Ohio	H	no no no			

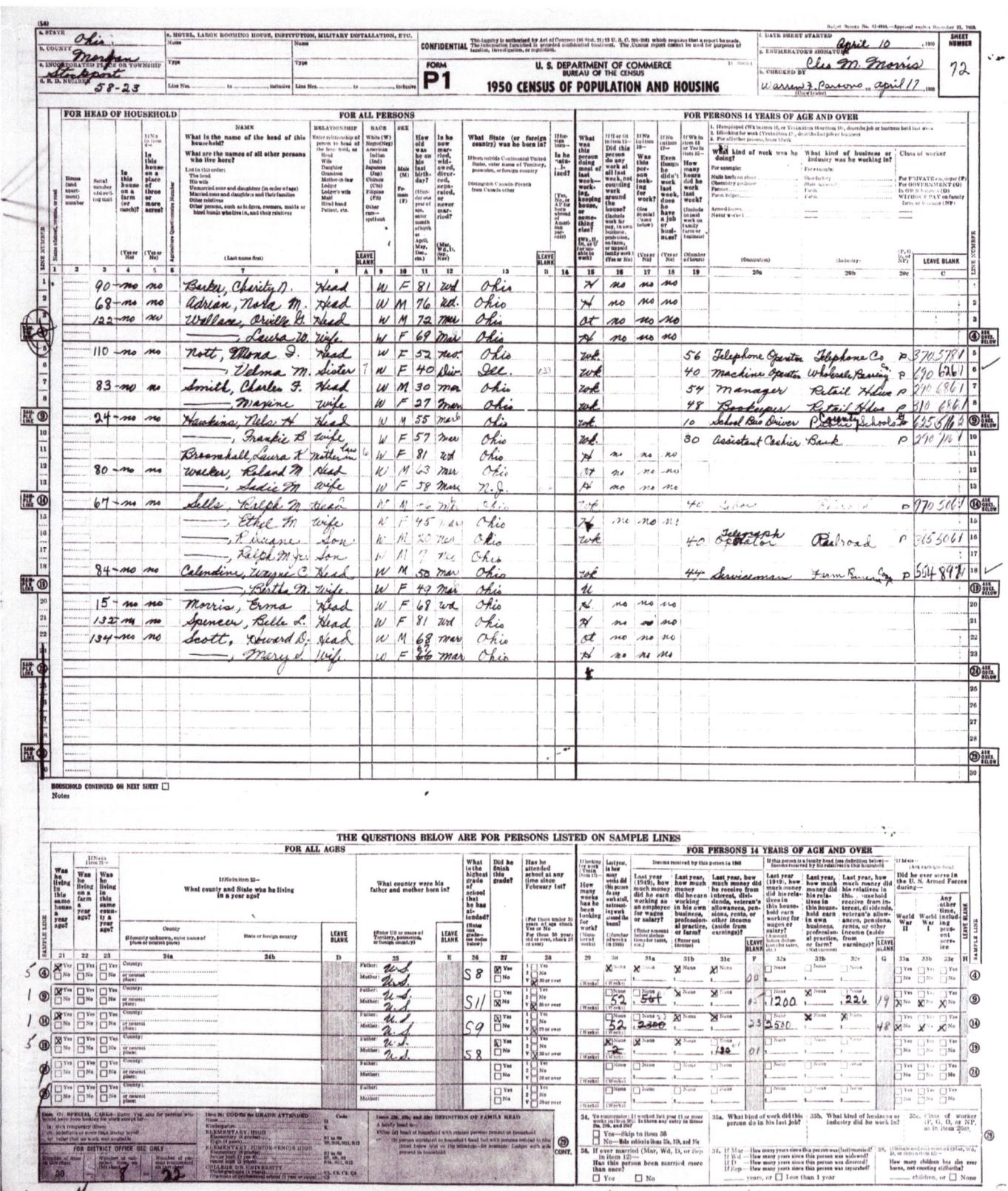

1950 CENSUS OF POPULATION AND HOUSING

State: Ohio
County: Morgan
Incorporated Place or Township: Stockport
E.D. Number: 58-23
Sheet Number: 73
Date Sheet Started: April 15, 1950
Enumerator's Signature: Cleo M. Morris

Line	Serial No.	Name	Relationship	Race	Sex	Age	Marital	Birthplace	Wk	Hrs	Occupation	Industry	Class
1	124	Gage, C. Richard	Head	W	M	27	mar	Ohio	wk	48	Office Manager	Farm Bureau	
2		—, Dorothy E.	Wife	W	F	28	mar	Ohio	wk	34	Primary Teacher	State School	
3		—, Lynne L.	Dau	W	F	2	nev	Ohio					
4	89	Cheadle, Hattie	Head	W	F	78	wd	Ohio	H				
5		—, Oscar	Son	W	M	53	nev	Ohio	wk	48	Farm Helper	Farm	NP
6		Rowland, Grace I.	Grand Dau	W	F	28	nev	Ohio	wk	40	Inspector	Roller Bearings Co.	
7	27	Faires, Wilfred L.	Head	W	M	26	mar	Ohio	wk	100	Prop	Restaurant	O
8		—, Betty J.	Wife	W	F	25	mar	Ohio	wk	40	L. Reporter	Newspaper	P
9	82	Chagnill, Wok J.	Head	W	M	89	wd	Ohio	H				
10	140	Dawson, Frank A.	Head	W	M	74	mar	Ohio	wk	20	Farmer	Home work	
11		—, Della	Wife	W	F	72	mar	Ohio	H	no no no			
12	51	Ross, J. Neil	Head	W	M	27	mar	Ohio	wk		Veterinary	Private Practice	O
13		—, MaryLou	Wife	W	F	27	mar	Ohio	H	no no no			
14		—, Betsy Jo	Dau	W	F	6	nev	Ohio					
15	53	Eddleblute, Clarence C.	Head	W	M	56	mar	Ohio	H	no no no			
16		—, Cora L.	Wife	W	F	55	mar						
17	4	Batchelor, Denny	Head	W	M	70	wd	Ohio	wk	10	Truck Hauler Transfer		O
18		—, Ray D.	Son	W	M	38	mar	Ohio	wk	58	Parts Salesman	Retail Hdw.	P
19		—, Ada	Dau-in-law	W	F	30	mar	Ohio	H	no no no			
20		—, Carol M.	Grand Dau	W	F	2	nev	Ohio					
21	39	Coles, Clyde C.	Head	W	M	29	mar	Ohio	wk	44	Carpenters Helper	Wholesale Bldg.	P
22		—, Audrey L.	Wife	W	F	27	mar	La.	H	no no no			
23	65	Smith, Frank M.	Head	W	M	43	Div	Ohio	wk	60	Attendant	Filling Station	P
24	144	Muse, Dale G.	Head	W	M	43	mar	Ohio	wk	48	Salesman	Retail Feed Store	P
25		—, Marjorie L.	Wife	W	F	39	mar	Ohio	wk	30	Cook	Cafe	P
26		—, Richard D.	Son	W	M	17	nev	Ohio	wk	18	Helper	Garage Repair	P
27		—, Jerry A.	Son	W	M	13	nev	Ohio					
28		—, Gary L.	Son	W	M	10	nev	Md.					
29	47	Porter, Wm H.	Head	W	M	76	wd	Ohio	wk	10	Carpenter Work	Private Home	P

1950 Census of Population and Housing

State: Ohio
County: Morgan
Incorporated Place: Stockport
E.D. Number: 58-23
Date: April 17
Enumerator: Cleo M. Morris
Sheet Number: 74

Line	House No.	Serial	On farm	Name (Last name first)	Relationship	Race	Sex	Age	Marital	Birthplace	Naturalized	Working?	Looking?	Hours	Kind of work	Industry	Class	Line
1	123	no	no	Wagner, Alfred C	Head	W	M	41	nev	Ohio		wk		16	Saw mill	Private	owner P 690307	1
2	107	no	no	Hollett, Lee	Head	W	M	47	mar	Ohio		wk						2
3				—, Helen	Wife	W	F	43	mar	Ohio		H	no no no					3
4	113	no	no	Cheadle, Belford P	Head	W	M	54	Wd	Ohio		wk		40	High School Teacher	County School	G 693888	4
5				—, Ida L	Mother	W	F	85	nev	Ohio		H						5
6	29	no	no	Morris, Earl E	Head	W	M	40	mar	Ohio		wk		45	Operate Bulldozer	Wholesale Lumber Co	P 522626	6
7				—, LaVerne	Wife	W	F	45	mar	Ohio		wk		45	Clerk	Retail Grocery	P 490636	7
8				—, Don	Son	W	M	16	nev	Ohio		ot	no no no					8
9	30	no	no	Mills, Ernest U	Head	W	M	45	mar	Ohio		wk		15	Drilling Machine	Private owner	G 559817	9
10				—, Helen K	Wife	W	F	41	mar	Ohio		wk		42	Clerk	Retail Grocery	P 490636	10
11	111	no	no	Stull, George D	Head	W	M	29	mar	Ohio		wk		40	Labor	Electric Co	P 970586	11
12				—, Inez M	Wife	W	F	33	mar	Ohio		wk		40	Factory worker	Timber	P 690358	12
13				Bowser Clyde R	Son	W	M	16	nev	Ohio		ot	no no no					13
14				Jerry A	Son	W	M	14	nev	Ohio		ot	no no no					14
15				Persons Transferred from JCB														15
16	901			Nickols, Doris E		1	2	46	1			1		16			524469	16
17				Persons Not Assigned to D.U.														17
18				Forney, Blanche		6	1	26	2			4						18
19				Creighton, J E		7	1	28	1			ow						19

Appendix K

Old Time Boatmen on the Muskingum River[178]

Researched by Benjamin P. Putnam in 1823 and copied by

Clyde K. Swift

1980

The following is a list of the names of all the Muskingum river keelboatmen that can be obtained by the writer [Benjamin Putnam], but like the list of keelboats, it is no doubt quite incomplete. Many of these men became prominent steamboat men and contributed much to the development of the navigation of the Ohio and Mississippi valleys:

David Anson, Baker, Absolom Boyd, Hercules Boyd, James Boyd, Hiram Burch, McC. Bell, James Blunt, John Burroughs, James Booker, Booths, Curtis, McC. Coleman, John Carpenter, William Carpenter, Daniel Clay, Stephen Davis, Freeman Davis, Hildrick Davis, Ed. Davis, Dudley Davis, Frederick Davis, John Davis, Simeon Manchester Devol Sr., Paul Ditenhaver, Joseph (Little Jo.) Devol, Bennet Devol, Simeon Devol, Tillinghast (Till) Devol, Dennis Devol, Stanton Devol, Joseph (Big Jo.) Devol, Evens, Frederick Erick, George W. Ebert, Even Evens, Ferrell, Randolph Fearing, John Farris, Mike Fink, Jacob Flake, Benjamin Godfrey, Simeon Girty, Samuel Godfrey, John Green, George Hahn, Michael Hahn, Frederick Hahn (Major), James Herron, William Helmick, Scudder Hart, Aaron Hart, Owen Hale, Isaac Newton Hook, Alexander Hahn, Israel[,?] Knott, Isaac Johnson, Thomas Johnson, William (Purdy Bill) Larison, John B. Lewis, Robert Leget, James Leget, John Lyons, George Michael, A. Z. Morris, William Parker, Adam Poe, Jacob Poe, Lemuel Pratt, Rearden Reese, Tice Ridenhour, Ryan, Stephen Roberts, Washington Scales, William Scales, Jesse Smith, Harry Stull, Nelson Stone, Stephen Stone, Anstin W. Sprague, William Silverthorn,

---

[178] *American Friend and Marietta Gazette*, October 9, 1823. Clyde K. Swift presented this list under the year "1823" in his research notes.

Lemuel Swift, John Tarrier, Talbot, Asa Travis, Harris White, Stephen West, Webster, and Williams.   —Benj P Putnam.

Of the men named in the foregoing list, the Boyds, the Hahns, the Caseys, Ayers, Scales Ridenhour, and Helmick were from Zanesville. The Davises were from Marietta and Lowell vicinities and Devols nearly all from Beverly and its vicinity. Clay was from Lowell, Fearing and Hart were from Marietta. The Johnsons, Evanses, [K]Notts, Godfreys, Legets, White, Swift and Webster were from Luke Chute[.] Travis, Coleman, Bell, and others from McConnelsville. [Captain Isaac N.] Hook [is] living near Windsor [Stockport] and nearly all the others resided somewhere on the Muskingum river and have descendants still living. It is a matter of much regret that the names of all the men who were connected with these pioneer boats could not be obtained for publication in this list.

www.ingramcontent.com/pod-product-compliance
Lightning Source LLC
Chambersburg PA
CBHW041707160426
43209CB00017B/1771